TEN OUT OF TEN

The first ten years of
Sgoil Chiùil na Gàidhealtachd

TERRY WILLIAMS

Sgoil Chiùil
na Gàidhealtachd

The National Centre of Excellence in Traditional Music

Published in June 2010 by Sgoil Chiùil na Gàidhealtachd
Pupil Residence
Plockton High School
Plockton IV52 8TU
www.musicplockton.org

Ten Out of Ten
The first ten years of Sgoil Chiùil na Gàidhealtachd

ISBN: 978-0-9565631-0-1

Design: Ronan Martin
Cover photograph: Cailean Maclean
Printed by Strath Print, Isle of Skye

The Highland
Council
Comhairle na
Gàidhealtachd

The National Centre of Excellence in Traditional Music is financed by
The Highland Council in partnership with the Scottish Government's
Department of Education & Lifelong Learning.

CONTENTS

FOREWORD

Peter Peacock

Being a Government Minister affords you the opportunity to make a difference. While agreeing to support and fund the traditional music school at Plockton would not be one of the biggest decisions I had a part in making, it is without question one of the most satisfying.

It was obvious from the very start, and a visit I made to the school, that this was real success in the making. So it has proved. I was treated to a wide display of talent in singing and a whole range of instruments.

The success of the school has contributed greatly to the wider success that this sector of music is enjoying, strengthening the confidence of those taking part, opening personal opportunities for them, and contributing to Scotland's wider reputation and success.

Our school system is by and large very successful, and local schools serve their communities well in music and a range of other subjects. However, there was a gap in what was being done nationally, and there was and is a case for youngsters who can benefit from a special setting in which to flourish, to be given that opportunity. Plockton provides that special setting for a particular group of talented musicians, but their experience and work spreads more widely and inspires a range of other schools.

Plockton is one of the real jewels in the crown of modern Scottish education. It sits there proudly with a range of other specialist schools focusing on other forms of music. When those schools get together, as I was privileged to witness just a couple of years ago in Strathpeffer, the result is of the highest quality. It makes me very proud indeed to have played a wee part in the process of their development.

Long may the success continue.

Peter Peacock was the Scottish Executive's Minister for Education in 1999.

FOREWORD

Bruce Robertson

When the Scottish Executive invited expressions of interest from Local Authorities for the Centres of Excellence programme, we in Highland felt that a Centre for Traditional Music was a pressing national requirement. Where better than Plockton, a wonderful West Highland location with strong Gaelic traditions and the excellent academic record of the High School?

The enthusiasm of Duncan Ferguson and Bert Richardson, who helped with the original bid and became part of the steering group, was infectious. Add to that the appointment of Dougie Pincock as Director and we were ready to invite applications!

And did we get applications? The quantity and quality of the applications that the Centre gets from across Scotland has confirmed just how right we all were to back this project. The success of the Centre has been a consequence of skilled, hard working students being motivated by outstanding tutors, among the best in Scotland.

The results have been stunning – young people gaining measurably in ability, confidence and qualifications; large numbers going on to the Royal Scottish Academy of Music and Drama and other studies; new performers arriving on the Scottish stage. And, of course – Young Scottish Traditional Music Award winners!

On a personal note, I will highlight my input to this project as one of the best things I ever did as Director in Highland. Along the way I have met some great young people, enjoyed their company, carried their instruments in Nova Scotia, and aye, shed a tear when they have performed. Never in my wildest dreams did I think Sgoil Chiùil na Gàidhealtachd would be the huge success it has been.

Bruce Robertson, OBE, was the Highland Council's Director of Education in 1999

PREFACE

In January 2010, the following report appeared in the *West Highland Free Press*.

The young musicians of Plockton took Glasgow's Royal Concert Hall by storm when the National Centre of Excellence in Traditional Music (Sgoil Chiùil na Gàidhealtachd) made its first official appearance at Celtic Connections.

There was hardly an empty seat in the Strathclyde Suite for the final concert of the TMSA Young Trad Tour, where Plockton's ten senior pupils had been allocated the first half of the programme. The seven-strong Young Trads' line up included three winners of the BBC Radio Scotland Young Traditional Musician of the Year as well as two graduates of Sgoil Chiùil. Ewan Robertson (guitar and vocals) was one of the Centre's very first intake in 2000, and won the Young Traditional Musician of the Year award in 2008. Daniel Thorpe (fiddle) went on to claim the 2010 title, the day after the concert! Prestigious company indeed for the teenagers.

Undaunted, they took to the stage like old hands. After the long, wintry journey from the north – with their fiddles and pipes and whistles and guitars and even a cello – they were going to make the most of the occasion. Three young pipers swept on to the stage, and within a few notes had the full attention of 500 people. Whoops and cheers met this fine start by Ewan Duncan, Catriona Gibb and Alexander Levack, setting the pattern for the rest of the show.

A fiddle and piano duet from Mhairi MacKinnon and Heather Shelley started slow and gentle, the two instruments singing as one. The set blossomed into a whirl of reels that demonstrated the formidable talent of these two young musicians. What's more,

8

they were clearly enjoying the experience. And so it continued, with songs from Amy Cameron, fine guitar accompaniment from Callum Forsyth, Jayne Paterson joining Mhairi on fiddle, and Duncan Bullivant bringing out his cello.

Without doubt the real show stopper was Natalie Chalmers, singing "The Alford Cattle Show". Her performance was a delight of words, music and mime as she conjured up the bothy loon proudly taking his beloved old mare to the fair, removing his sark to join in the games, drinking too much, dancing too much, falling into the arms of a girl…. As chorus followed chorus, voices from the floor gradually joined in, until by the time the poor lad was finally caught and "merrit", Natalie had the whole audience singing along. A real tradition bearer in full voice – and still under 18!

It was astonishing to see such mature, confident performances from such young players. Through reels and slow airs, dances and laments, not a note fell out of place. They might have missed Burns Night, said the students, but they'd sing "Auld Lang Syne" anyway – and their new, refreshing arrangement met with noisy approval.

The Young Trads, having spun their own amazing magic through the second half, called the Plockton group back on stage for a "big band" set. In a white-knuckle performance, Ruairidh MacMillan – fiddler and 2009 Young Traditional Musician of the Year – kept cranking up the pace. The youngsters rose superbly to the challenge, fingers flying right to the very last note. At the final bow there was a broad grin on every face.

We've come to expect technical brilliance and musical excellence from the students of Sgoil Chiùil, but this concert has taken them to a new level. The Celtic Connections success is a real milestone and couldn't be better timed, as the Centre approaches its tenth anniversary.

It was an emotional occasion for Dougie Pincock, Director since the launch of the project in 2000.

"I felt as if the whole ten years was distilled into that one 50 minute set," he said. "Everything we do with and for them was there on that day. They were organised, professional...just perfect. The only twinge was I wanted to be up there playing with them!"

This book celebrates the first decade of a remarkable musical journey.

CHAPTER I

To Begin at the Beginning...

The National Centre of Excellence in Traditional Music was established at Plockton High School in May 2000. The Centre is open to any secondary school age student resident in Scotland, and aims to provide the highest possible quality of tuition and an all-round, in-depth experience of all aspects of Scottish traditional music. The Centre is nominally funded for 23 places as a result of the Executive's Best Value Review of 2005.
Annual Report to Scottish Executive's Education Department, 2006/07

The right people were in the right place at the right time.

The time was 1999 and the Scottish Executive had their eye on the new millennium. Putting £5 million into a pot labelled Excellence Fund, they contacted the education department of every local authority in the country. What they offered was start-up funding from the Scottish Executive's Education Department – to be administered by local councils – for the creation of National Centres of Excellence in any educational field. (Since 2007 the NCETM has been directly funded by the Highland Council.)

What they generated in one corner of the West Highlands was an explosion of energy that would lead to a unique musical experiment.

When the call for tenders reached the Highland Council Offices in Inverness, Director of Education, Bruce Robertson, jumped into action. Together with his colleague, Bert Richardson, Advisor in Music to the Council, Bruce had been aware for some time of a growing pool of young traditional musicians all over Scotland. They were the result of a movement that began in 1981 on the island of Barra in the Western Isles. Fèis Bharraigh was the first community-run Gaelic cultural festival offering young people top class tuition from well-known working musicians, within reach of their own homes. Music, song, dance, customs and arts were all included and the idea proved so popular that communities throughout the Gàidhealtachd and beyond had followed Barra's example. The national network of Fèisean nan Gàidheal was now producing young players ideally suited to the environment of a National Centre of Excellence in Traditional Music.

The time was perfect. What was more, Bruce also knew the right place.

Plockton, on the west coast of Ross-shire, lies at the heart of a widespread community renowned for its support of traditional music and Gaelic culture. The village curls round a pine-and-crag-sheltered bay, turning its back to the prevailing weather that sweeps in from the mountains of Skye, a few sea miles to the west. The main street is fringed with water's-edge gardens, palm trees sway in the breeze, sailing boats dance at their moorings, and seals lounge about the scattered islands of Loch Carron. Several times each day a train chunters round the far side of the bay along the single-track line that meanders from Inverness to Kyle of Lochalsh. It halts at a tiny station above the village, just a few minutes' walk from Plockton High School.

In the Rector's office, Duncan Ferguson interrupted his paperwork to answer the phone. It was Bruce Robertson, with a question. Would Duncan be interested in hosting a centre of traditional music at the school? Most definitely he would, was the instant reaction.

Through its previous Rector, the great Gaelic poet Sorley MacLean, and Duncan's own track record, Plockton High School was already well respected for its commitment to Gaelic language and culture. It also had a very strong tradition of piping. Tutor Iain MacFadyen had nurtured a steady flow of fine young pipers, many of whom had gone on to make a name for themselves in the wider world. With a catchment area that stretched from Shieldaig and Applecross in the north to Glenelg and Arnisdale in the south, Plockton – like many other Highland secondary schools – had residential accommodation for students from remoter communities, for whom daily travel was not feasible. It was the ideal place for the new project. The deadline for applications was looming. On Bruce's instructions, Duncan and Bert set to work.

The next few weeks were a whirl of meetings, discussions and writing as they researched, drafted and re-drafted their proposal. They went to Edinburgh and spoke with members of the Scottish Executive; to Glasgow, where Douglas Academy in Bearsden had been running a music school for over 20 years; back to Edinburgh to see how Broughton High School managed their music centre. Both these well-established enterprises would also bid for – and win – funding as centres of excellence in music, as would another new proposal at Dyce Academy in Aberdeen. However, none was to be solely, or even substantially, dedicated to traditional music. What the Plockton team were trying to do was an absolute first and they wanted to get it right.

When the news came that their bid had been approved, delight soon gave way to alarm. In a very short time indeed they had to sort out accommodation, teaching facilities, and most important of all, appoint a Director. What exactly did they need such a person to do? This was to be a residential centre where talented young musicians could come and live, be educated and be exposed to a top-quality experience in the traditional music of Scotland. Bert drew up a wish list of criteria for both job and incumbent.

"This person doesn't exist," he thought.

"Dougie Pincock's arrival on the scene at this stage was nothing short of providential!"
Bert Richardson, former Advisor in Music to Highland Council

At BBC Radio Scotland in Glasgow, Dougie Pincock was helping Archie Fisher present his live weekly music programme, Travelling Folk, when an item arrived for the diary section of the show. He read out the advert for a brand new post in Plockton, tucked away on the north west coast. His reaction was broadcast to the nation.

"That would make a nice wee job for somebody somewhere at some point."
Dougie Pincock

"At the time there was no inkling that he had his sights set on the job and there had never been a precedent for such a position. It seemed miles away, not only from the Scottish traditional music hub in the Lowlands, but also it seemed like a geographical outpost, far away from the potential work centres. Dougie must have thought hard about the potential life changing decision as he was, literally in a way, going to have to invent his own job."
Archie Fisher, Presenter, BBC Radio Scotland Travelling Folk

Later, Dougie looked over the full requirements of the position: a track record as a performer, experience of teaching traditional music to young people; experience of working in residential situations and schools; good contacts; a public profile – he had all those.

Dougie had learned to play the bagpipes at primary school and had been travelling the traditional music road ever since. He'd been a piper with Battlefield Band, a Fèis tutor for many years; he'd taught at the National Piping Centre and the Royal Scottish Academy of Music and Drama (RSAMD); he'd been involved in the Easterhouse Arts Project. He knew people in all corners of the traditional music world, and they knew him – and so did the music-listening public through his radio work with Archie.

His one lack was "budget management". But he could count, and he knew that if you got a certain amount of money you shouldn't spend any more than that or you'd be in trouble – yes, he could do budget management. What's more, his own family budget would be greatly helped by a regular income. So he applied for the position of Director at the soon-to-be-established National Centre of Excellence in Traditional Music, Sgoil Chiùil na Gàidhealtachd.

He got the job.

CHAPTER II

A Rocky Start

Director's responsibilities:
Budget management • CD production • Performance schedule
Programming • Weekend music activities • Groupwork teaching
Individual teaching of own instrument • Student welfare • Parental liaison
School liaison • Staff development and review • Quality Assurance
Auditions • Advertising • Development planning • External relations

Dougie was appointed on 2nd May 2000. The new school year would begin in August. There were already a few applications for places, but no curriculum. That was the Director's first task and Dougie soon realised it had been cunningly anticipated. At the job interview, each candidate had been asked to present their view of how a centre of excellence should work. To this day, the Centre's curriculum is based on the ideas Dougie put forward at his interview.

There was no pile-carpeted, French-windowed executive suite waiting for the Director of the National Centre of Excellence in

Traditional Music. He prepared that first curriculum at a table in a hastily-emptied storage space in the Pupil Residence. A proper office would be available as soon as the building had been altered to accommodate the Centre. Those years as a working musician on the road with the Battlefield Band were going stand him in good stead – Dougie knew how to make the most of things and get on with the job. As it happened, he was going to be doing a lot of that over the next six months.

> **"He started with a desk in what used to be a cupboard, a pad of paper and a pen, and the order to make a music school."**
> Anita Hurding, Clerical Assistant

Dougie was greatly encouraged at this period by the support of his steering group – Duncan Ferguson, Bert Richardson, and Laurence Young, Area Education Manager for Skye and Lochalsh at the time. Their experience was invaluable in guiding the new Director's first steps. A bonus for Dougie was Laurence's personal involvement in traditional music through Fèis Lochabair. It was reassuring to have someone who understood the huge transition from outside world into the maze of the education system.

> **"Laurence became my line manager. He could put himself in my shoes and see things the way I was looking at them, because he had experience of traditional musicians and wasn't confined to looking at it from within the educational perspective...He was extremely supportive because of his involvement in education, but also his support for traditional music as well – he wanted to make this thing work."**
> Dougie Pincock

They all wanted to make it work, and their combined knowledge and enthusiasm made sure that it did.

Along with his willingness to learn new ropes, Dougie's make-it-work approach won him vital support among the Residence staff. Matron Cathy Taylor had arrived at Plockton High School in 1983, when around 70 youngsters were bursting the seams of the residential building. Since those days, with improved transport throughout the region, more pupils could travel home each night. By the time Duncan and Bert were talking persuasively to the Scottish Executive in Edinburgh, the Residence had just 16 boarders, and its future looked uncertain. The arrival of the Music School students would be a lifeline, and Cathy was ready to welcome them with open arms.

By "some devilish cantrip slicht" as he put it, Dougie managed to produce a teaching programme, find some tutors, and recruit ten pupils in time for the beginning of term. The first challenge had been met. There were plenty more to come.

Renovation work started. The whole ground floor of the Residence was to be altered, at no little disruption to the existing inhabitants. There would be a proper Director's office, a music room, storage for instruments, and a library. The existing cloakrooms would be converted into practice rooms, a recording studio, and a piping room. That was the plan. It went agley with a vengeance when the building was found to be riddled with asbestos. The place was uninhabitable.

It was not a happy start. The Residence's already precarious situation looked hopeless, and it must have seemed to the High School boarders that this small group of musical strangers had effectively destroyed their living space. But the newcomers had problems too. Without a building, the Centre of Excellence had no home at all, and the project looked doomed to fail before it had even started. But the steering group weren't giving up so soon. Laurence Young started making phone calls.

"Especially important at that point was Laurence's experience on the residential side. He was Education Manager at the time with responsibility for all school hostels in Skye and Lochalsh."
Dougie Pincock

By the time school opened, Sabhal Mòr Ostaig, the Gaelic college at the south end of the Isle of Skye, had come to the rescue with bed, breakfast and dinner for the students, and even a small separate flat for Cathy. To attend school in Plockton, the pupils had a 30-mile journey by bus at each end of every day. It meant an early start for everyone and a very long day for the music students, whose special studies took place mostly after normal school hours.

It was hardly an ideal introduction, but as far as possible the agreed teaching programme was launched. The High School music department lent practice rooms for individual daytime tuition, and Dougie followed the students over to Skye to oversee the evening groupwork and practice sessions.

> **"I felt very sorry for them because we had to get them up so early. We had to come and prepare breakfast because the Sabhal Mòr Ostaig staff weren't on duty at that time. So we used to get up at five o'clock, and they had to be up before seven."**
> Cathy Taylor, former Matron of Pupil Residence

The first six months were tough on everyone. Nevertheless, the Centre's first students remember that time with some affection. The bus journeys may have been tedious, but it was great to wander down to the shore at the weekends. Getting up so early was unpopular, especially with the boys. They were housed in the old part of the college, and had to get up half an hour earlier than the girls, to walk across the campus for their breakfast.

> **"That was wild ...you were up early, then travelling on the bus for a good hour, then you were in school all day, then the bus trip on the way home...you had your study to do, and your practice to do, then you had groupwork to do as well."**
> Ewan Robertson, former student

Cathy and her Assistant Matron, Shona McGuinness, went out of their way to support the youngsters, keeping up small, homely rituals that helped everyone feel secure. Shona spent evenings and nights at the college, returning to her own family on the mainland during the day. En route, she went shopping for supper-time food.

She knew the children loved their supper, and a bit of asbestos wasn't going to get in the way of their "wee treats". It had disrupted quite enough already.

For parents, the flitting must have caused more than a little anxiety. Having committed their children to a totally untried and untested educational experiment, and into the care of strangers a long way from home, they were told that due to unforeseen circumstances and for an unspecified period of time, their offspring would actually be staying in a college of further education, miles from Plockton. In addition they would be spending two hours a day travelling by bus between school and accommodation. Hardly anyone changed their mind, thanks to the confidence inspired by Dougie and staff in both the Residence and the High School.

Ten years on, it remains a source of wonder to Dougie that parents are willing to put their children in his care! Although he had been able to tick most of the boxes for his job interview, being responsible for not only the musical education but also the welfare of ten teenagers was a whole new experience. Cathy watched quietly and with approval as he and his charges found their respective and collective feet. She admired Dougie's enthusiasm and drive, and appreciated his honesty. This well-known figure from the world of traditional music wasn't slow to ask for advice when a student's well-being depended on him.

> **"He was very good. I admired him – he hadn't worked before with children but he had a family of his own and I think that makes a difference. He was very good with them. I'm sure there was the odd one saying 'Dougie was on to me about something'. I used to say if we didn't care about you we wouldn't give you a telling off. It's not that we don't love you, it's what you do that we don't like."**
> Cathy Taylor

Dougie hands a large part of the credit to the students themselves. If they hadn't responded so well, the whole project could have fallen apart, despite the best efforts of the adults involved. The older students seemed to take everything in their stride, and looked after the younger ones. Only one youngster didn't manage to settle – the others displayed remarkable equanimity. They had come for the music, and so long as music was what they got, they were quite happy. And they did enjoy living by the sea!

> **"It was an adventure, and there was good paddling to be had! I think it wasn't really what everybody expected because we were based in Skye, and that meant we were doing a lot of travelling every day. I think for the wee ones it was very hard. Only nine of us...we could look after each other in a really nice way. Well, there were ten at first and then a boy went home. He was young and it was just too much, poor loon. He was a great fiddle player. It was crazy times."**
> Gillian Fleetwood, former student

Dougie was eager to get the Centre properly up and running, and he longed to get back to Plockton. Not least, he wanted his own family around him again. His wife, Gillian, and their two children had been waiting in Glasgow while the Music School found its feet. At last, towards the end of January 2001, the building work was finished and Sgoil Chiùil na Gàidhealtachd came home.

> **"We got a very good report after we'd been at Sabhal Mòr Ostaig...praising their behaviour and everything for the time we were there. So I sent a copy to every parent, just to show that everything was not as bad as sometimes it might seem!"**
> Cathy Taylor

The return to Plockton was a huge relief for everyone, but it marked a crucial point in the life of the Residence, and the start of a balancing act that has never stopped. How much easier for the students to get up and have breakfast at a reasonable time with a short walk to the High School, and how much pleasanter be in the Residence within minutes of finishing the last lesson of the day. The "old hands" enjoyed being back in their own space, with their own cook who knew their likes and dislikes. It was good to have the familiar village on the doorstep again. There had been many changes in the building during their months of exile. Thanks to the Centres of Excellence Fund (and, in a perverse way, to the asbestos) everyone had better sleeping quarters, fresh paint, new carpets…yet much of the original Residence had been converted into facilities for the Music School. It would take some getting used to, for both staff and pupils.

That first group of music students came from places like Speyside, Aberdeenshire, Inverness, Perth and Bishopbriggs, their different accents mingling with the Director's own rich Scots. They brought with them their fiddles, accordions, singing voices, whistles, guitars, bagpipes and clàrsachs, along with their joy in making good music. They were already accomplished young players, keen to learn more. They were working hard, having a lot of fun, giving and receiving a great deal of mutual support. In the short space of time they'd been together, a remarkable level of respect and affection had sprung up between students, Director and tutors. The unexpected nature of their first months at the school had helped bind them into a close-knit group.

"I think because it was the first year and there were only nine of us, we were really close, especially by the end."
Ewan Robertson

However, every student who enrols at Sgoil Chiùil becomes a member of three distinct yet interrelated communities. First, they join a group of talented young traditional musicians – up to 23 at any one time, aged from 11 to 18. Second, they enter the High School's roll of around 300 pupils, for a full mainstream course of academic study. Last, but by no means least, they take their place in the intimate community of the Residence. They are expected to play a full part in all three. It's a tall order for a new kid on the pressure-ridden teenage block, especially one who's just left home for the first time.

"I was seventeen. There's a lot to take in. Being at a new school for one thing. Being at a new school and under the

22

microscope because it's the first year...It was an unknown
quantity at the time and everybody was 'what are you doing
in our school, in our Residence where we all live?' Some
people had lived in that Residence for five years."
Gillian Fleetwood

Dougie, Cathy and Duncan were anxious to avoid a split between
Music School and High School pupils. They knew that a happy,
balanced home environment – in this case, life in the Residence –
was vital.

"Because of the way they spend their lives, they are a little
bit different. They don't have 'Music School' written on their
foreheads but for a lot of the time, by the nature of what
they do, they are different. I think we are always working at
integration, to be sure that our staff and pupils don't exclude
them, but also educating them that they have to appreciate
that they are part of a larger whole."
Duncan Ferguson

Once again, Laurence Young was able to provide invaluable support.

"Laurence...had a lot of experience of the residential
complications, procedures, rules, regulations, hoops to jump
through. He was invaluable in helping us get these new
students into the residential side of things."
Dougie Pincock

It wasn't easy, but with every passing year the barriers have been
crumbling. Now, the advantages of having a Music School on the
premises usually outweigh the drawbacks, and Plockton's Residence
is home to a happy bunch of young people.

"Integrating these two groups of pupils has taken a while to
get sorted. They now co-exist well. They're a long way from
home, at a vulnerable age, making career decisions, subject
choices. It's a steep learning curve, particularly for me and
other music staff not used to that kind of thing."
Dougie Pincock

The first breakthrough was made, unsurprisingly, by the music itself. A "wee concert in the dining hall" became a significant landmark, remembers Cathy. "They proved themselves," she recalls. Now everyone could see what was going on behind the fancy name in this National Centre of Excellence in Traditional Music and they were impressed. From that time, Plockton High School has taken great pride in having Sgoil Chiùil na Gàidhealtachd under its wing, and the Centre has gone on to make a growing contribution to the High School's musical scene.

"It's great for me. If I have visitors from Finland next week and I want a ceilidh, I can have a top class ceilidh within ten minutes!"
Duncan Ferguson, Rector, Plockton High School

CHAPTER III

The Daily Round

All pupils of the Centre study two disciplines, and receive one 54 minute period per week of individual instruction in each of these disciplines. These two periods are classroom extraction periods...tutors devise a programme of instruction which is tailored to the needs of the individual student. Students are involved in their own learning, and often select specific material or types of material they wish to learn. The Centre students... follow an evening programme which combines their music programme with the normal Residence activities. This programme is monitored very closely and reviewed regularly.
Annual Report 2006/07

Dougie forged ahead with his teaching programme, weaving the three strands of music, education and welfare into a secure framework within which the young musicians could thrive.

A decade later that original structure stands firm, enhanced by a number of additions and improvements over the years. It all makes for a demanding schedule that commits students to a minimum basic ten hours of active involvement in traditional music from Monday to Thursday each week. Individual instrumental tuition – an hour on each of their first and second study instruments – means missing two High School classes a week, and of course catching up on them afterwards. The remaining eight hours are devoted to groupwork and supervised practice after normal school hours. All this comes on top of a full day of academic lessons and the homework that goes with them – and that's not counting the Music Weekends, the CD recordings, or the 35-40 performances that are squeezed into each year!

> **"Oidhche mhath agus cadal math agus eiridh trath 's a'mhadainn – good night, sleep well and get up early in the morning."**
> Cathy Taylor

The day begins with breakfast and the usual reluctant last-minute rush to get out of the Residence and across to the High School in time for the first lesson. By nine o'clock the tumult has died down, the Director and his Administrative Assistant have opened up the Music School office, and the everyday work of the Residence is underway – cleaning, cooking, working out menus, dealing with paperwork.

The first tutor arrives – complete with overnight bag, briefcase and instrument cases – sounding the main door buzzer that will punctuate the rest of the day with its calls for attention, as pupils flit between High School and Residence for their individual lessons. That buzzer haunts Shona McGuinness, who became Matron when Cathy retired in 2003 (the position is now "Branch Manager").

> **"They're in and out constantly, not in High School all day, like any other Residence. We're the only Residence that has this constant in and out. We have to check them in."**
> Shona McGuinness, Branch Manager, Pupil Residence

There are greetings, coffee, brief discussions, a sharing of news, laughter. Then work. A pipe tune filters through to the kitchen where the cook is preparing the day's food. At her desk, Shona hears the sound of a fiddle in the next room. Cleaners polish floors to the strains of a Gaelic song. A visitor is struck by the daytime peace in this place, compared with the hubbub of conventional school life just a few hundred metres away. It's an illusion. In the office, Dougie and Anita Hurding keep up an astonishing pace – fielding phone calls, writing reports, sending emails, arranging meetings, discussing lessons, pupils, problems and plans.

> **"There's more and more demand that people want to see outcomes for funding. They want to see things being evaluated constantly. That puts an awful lot of administrative pressure on the place, and can take away from the time people have to devote to teaching music."**
> Jack Evans, Tutor

For the first couple of years, Dougie struggled on his own to keep up with the ever-growing administration. A burden lifted from his shoulders with the appointment of Sarah Houston as Clerical Assistant, followed by Anita in 2003. On a day-to-day level, Anita's priority is to make space for Dougie to function effectively as Director.

> **"It needs somebody to manage the place so he can be Director, have the big creative ideas…"**
> Anita Hurding

The more creative ideas, the more work. Anita has built up a formidable workload for herself, adding administrative excellence to the Centre's list of merits. Like any undercurrent, much of her office work is unseen, but if it stopped the results would soon be noticed!

> **"Anita has been a lynchpin of the whole thing, more or less since she stepped in the door. It's just incredible what she's done, not just in terms of her ability to do the job, but her ability to develop the role and also look at what other**

things could be done. Anita underpins the administration of everything. It's all very well me having ideas, but somebody has to have the role of putting these ideas into practice. She works way above and beyond the level of her job description...I cannae stop her, actually. The level of commitment she's shown to the project over the years has been phenomenal...Above all else, she takes a pride in her work. She wants to do the best job she can, all the time. That sets her apart..."
Dougie Pincock

In addition to her duties in the office, Anita has worked in the Residence, has toured with the students and helped with concerts.

"I've been in a band, been on tour myself so I know what's going on, what the pressures are...I can understand both sides of the story between Residence and Music School if there are conflicting demands...Accompanying the students on trips, you're interacting with them in a different way, eating in a restaurant, travelling, coping with the odd crisis."
Anita Hurding

Going the extra mile seems to be an intrinsic feature of this remarkable place. The source can be traced to the Director's office. The student handbook declares that "the Director is 'Mr Pincock' when he is wearing a tie, and 'Dougie' on less formal occasions". The pupils are liable to compromise happily with "Mr P".

Working with Mr P requires stamina and a steady nerve. He is a forger of ideas, with the energy to bring them to fruition. Having spent some time in a military pipe band, he knows the value of discipline and hard work. He demands the highest standards from everyone around him, but he does it with a twinkle in his eye and doesn't hesitate to give praise where it's due. It works. What's more, tie or no tie, Dougie Pincock remains the same hands-on, get-the-job-done person who saw the project through its first tentative months.

If the administrative workload threatens to spill over, he'll cheerfully handle a bed-and-breakfast booking for a tutor before hurrying off to rehearse the students for an important gig. Without accommodation the tutor can't teach the students, who in turn won't be able to perform the music at the concert, which is a vital part of their Sgoil Chiùil experience. So Dougie makes sure it happens. And his attitude spreads throughout the school, from staff to tutors to pupils.

On the eve of an important concert, after weeks of frantic preparation that has pushed everyone to the limit, Dougie pauses with a grin. "The lid's on. For the first time in weeks, everything's under control." Five minutes later, he dashes back into the office and grabs his jacket, the grin turning to laughter. "Lid's off. I forgot to collect the packed lunches."

An inspector of schools might comment that such tasks are not a productive use of the Director's time. But in the quest for all-round excellence – successful learners, effective contributors, confident individuals, responsible citizens – the pupils of Sgoil Chiùil could have no better example than the combined dedication of Mr P and Ms Hurding.

"The reward? It's a huge privilege to be working with these kids and to be part of their development...I absolutely love it. Everybody gives 50 times more than they have to."
Anita Hurding

The biggest single administrative challenge is balancing the pupils' instrumental lessons with their academic studies. All the tutors are juggling other commitments, fitting Plockton visits into their own busy calendars. They can't guarantee to be available on the same day every week. In addition, it's important to vary the High School subject lessons missed for music tuition, and to avoid any tests or laboratory sessions or field trips. All in all, timetabling the individual lessons is an administrative nightmare.

Anita's secret weapon is communication. The tutors tell her which day they will be in Plockton. The High School teachers tell her which sessions they don't want the pupils to miss. She matches everything up and passes the timetable to the students. Disruption is forever lurking in the wings, be it through illness, a late train, the weather, or a puncture. If a replacement tutor can be contacted, maybe the lesson can take place after all. If not, re-scheduling is the only option and Anita breaks off what she was hoping to get done in the next hour…

> **"I don't actually meet with the High School staff very often. I put out a weekly grid with the pupils' names and the school periods, for teachers to mark in when they've got National Assessment Board tests, geography field trips, or essential practical work…of course, every teacher wants every pupil in every lesson of theirs, so it's an ongoing negotiation. It works quite well and they are quite good at picking up the phone to me as well. It's a constant juggling act."**
> Anita Hurding

Contact between Music School and High School has been close from the start, and Dougie attends weekly meetings of the High School's Senior Management Team. The small group of music students places disproportionate demands on both establishments and the way they interact. Once again, communication in large quantities has been the key to a happy partnership.

> **"The whole administration of timetabling and programming lessons is a huge task…There have to be a lot of links between the two school offices."**
> Duncan Ferguson

> **"We have to be very flexible in our approach to timetabling – it does cause problems, for the tutors, for us, for the kids, for the High School. But it's the price we feel we have to pay to get these tutors in here, and we will continue to pay that price, not only financially but administratively. Because they are great."**
> Dougie Pincock

CHAPTER IV

Those Who Teach

Since its inception in May 2000, the Centre has gained a national and international reputation as a provider of the highest quality secondary education in Traditional Music. The Centre has assembled an extremely high quality tutor team consisting of some of the leading practitioners in the field who have a national and international reputation. This has been a key factor in attracting young people to apply for the Centre, and also in establishing the Centre's credibility within the traditional music community.

Annual Report 2006/07

The tutors have been a cornerstone of Sgoil Chiùil na Gàidhealtachd from the start. The Steering Group made a policy decision – with national excellence as the goal, students must have tuition of the very highest quality. It would require a significant portion of the budget, but the credibility of the Centre depended on the excellence of the musicians it produced. There was a considerable amount of public money in the project purse and the watchful eye of their sponsors would, quite correctly, be on them. Attracting the right tutors was vital. Thanks to his years on the performance circuit and his involvement with the Fèis movement, Dougie knew who they were and where to contact them.

He wanted brilliant performers steeped in the tradition of their craft. He wanted players and singers who could transmit their knowledge and enthusiasm to his group of talented, hard-pressed, young people. He wanted working musicians who could talk about life as it really was in the world of traditional music. The Centre would do everything possible to help these busy people make the weekly journey to Plockton – pay them well for their work, cover their travel expenses and overnight accommodation, offer flexible teaching hours.

It was a big investment, and it paid dividends. Most of the tutors teach regularly in other settings, for example during the Fèisean – a week here, a week there – but the only place in which most of them are accessible on a regular basis is at the National Centre of Excellence in Traditional Music. From all over Scotland during the past ten years, some of the finest traditional musicians in the country have been jumping on trains, boarding ferries, crossing bridges, travelling the roads and the miles, converging on Plockton to pass the tunes and songs of their heritage to the next generation. They come and go like a weekly tide, flowing in for a day or two, bringing a wealth of learning to their pupils and extra income to the local community, as they bed-and-breakfast in the village or lunch-and-dinner at the Plockton Inn.

> **"There's no doubt that for them all it's a labour of love.
> There is a clear commitment – it's master and apprentice…
> There is that sense of the great performers being able to
> share their talent with this new generation. The youngsters
> respond and the tutors are getting a real pleasure of passing
> on and seeing these youngsters coming on."**
> Duncan Ferguson

These musicians from "all the airts and pairts", as Dougie puts it, share his deep commitment to the ethos of the Centre. A singing teacher will drop in on a groupwork session, to see how they're getting on with a song she's been teaching one of the band. High School test dates have been changed at the last minute? No problem, the accordion lesson needn't be missed – it's shuffled into the gap between dinner and practice time, and the tutor will stay over.

> **"They're all amazing...It's such a big deal to be taught by Andy Thorburn...Some of them stay over and they're really nice...They do things because they want to, because they are here for us."**
> Amy, Kim, Mischa and Nikki, current students

Fiddle • Pipes • Clàrsach • Accordion • Cello • Guitar • Mandolin
Flute • Whistle • Scots song • Gaelic song • Bouzouki • Piano • Theory

---

All pupils concentrate on two disciplines – a first and second study. They audition on their primary instrument, which becomes their first study, but an equal teaching time of one class period a week is devoted to each. This makes the system very flexible. If someone's second study improves more than the first, it's no problem to swap them round. Students have even gone on to further courses with an instrument that began in Plockton as a second study. What's more, the second study can change from year to year. Pupils can try different instruments, perhaps one they've never come across before and would like to explore. For pupils in S3 to S6, the second study splits and they spend half the session doing a course in accompaniment and harmony. Finally, in the spirit of opening all possible doors, everyone is also encouraged to sing, normally as part of groupwork – even those who have never contemplated their own voice as an instrument!

"Singing…it was great. Since then I've always sung, always had it as something else to do. I'm not a first class singer in the same way as somebody with first choice would be, but to get over the fear was very brilliant, and something I'm very grateful for."
Gillian Fleetwood

No matter what the instrument, tuition comes from a professional, working musician. The many stand-by tutors are also working musicians. And the guests who come in to give workshops or lectures for the Music Weekends are working musicians too. As teachers and performers, they bring the reality of life as a traditional musician right into the heart of Sgoil Chiùil's sheltered environment, leaving their pupils with few illusions.

"It's difficult to make a living as a musician of any kind…It's something you have to work very, very hard at building for a long time."
Jack Evans

Students hear repeatedly that the market for traditional performers is small. Just as the pupils of Sgoil Chiùil are a tiny proportion of the country's talented young traditional players, so the people teaching them are only the tip of a very large iceberg. There are many, many good musicians enjoying and sharing traditional music in pubs, halls and gatherings throughout Scotland and beyond, while their main source of income comes from whatever the "day job" might be. It's a valuable insight, the more potent for coming from people the young folk respect, admire and have come to trust through the privilege of one-to-one tuition.

"I think the attitude should always be that you're learning music for the love of the music and the fun you can have with it, sharing it, playing with friends. If it happens that you go off and join a band and become a professional, good luck. For me it's all about the love and the understanding of it. That's the important thing."
Iain MacFarlane, Tutor

It's hardly surprising, given the prodigious talent that finds its way to Sgoil Chiùil, that some of the early students have overcome the odds and carved themselves quite a prominent niche in the crowded professional world. Some combine performing with teaching, either privately or within the school system.

> **"Doing what we do as musicians is not always easy, and I have to juggle quite a lot. I can't do as much gigging as I want because I'm teaching, and I can't always teach as much as I want because I'm committed to a gig...but it's very rewarding and I love it."**
> Gillian Fleetwood

A very few have become full-time performers. While studying fiddle and pipes at Sgoil Chiùil, Ewan Robertson also played the guitar, which has since taken over his life. Among other successes, he helped form the award-winning band, Breabach.

> **"I've not spent more than three nights in one place this year so far – I wouldn't have it any other way. I've travelled all over the place: China, Shanghai, Australia, Canada. We're going to India, France, Spain. We did a month's tour in England with Breabach. That was fantastic, great gigs, great audiences. We did a month's European tour in October."**
> Ewan Robertson

Although the majority of Plockton's music students are keen to move on to further music studies, not every pupil wants to be a full-time musician. Some may become joiners, lawyers, builders, policemen and women, teachers, linguists or nurses. As far as Sgoil Chiùil is concerned, all are equally valid and valued paths, so long as the music goes too.

> **"Our philosophy of not pushing people always down the music line is at odds with some of the other music centres, where people go specifically to be a musician. That's the classical way. It's fine – just a different approach."**
> Dougie Pincock

"There was no pressure to become a professional musician, but the immersion in music means you have it for the rest of your life. It's not wasted."
Suzanne Houston, former student

For every student, whatever the road ahead, musical excellence is the aim and full commitment is expected. In return for their tutor's personal attention and professional expertise, pupils must be punctual, polite, organised and – not least – communicative. If they have a problem, the tutor needs to know. If they want to explore a certain style of music, it's worth talking about it. Lessons are followed up by set work to be completed by the next week. Practice (or the lack of it) will show in progress – or the lack of it!

"To have fun with music, they've got to work hard and there's a lot of hours of hardship to get the enjoyment... but once it's there, it's there. Music adds to your character. Even if you never do anything with it and you go off to be a doctor, it's such an important part of your character."
Iain MacFarlane

There is a great deal of hard work. There is also a huge amount of fun. These tutors are "kent names", and have probably already been an inspiration from afar. The sheer delight of having a childhood hero to yourself for an hour each week, with the chance of learning all they have to teach you – that's a very special thing indeed.

"Kids playing rock music, they're never going to meet their heroes. Yet here we do it week in, week out...It's just great, it's special music. There's a real community spirit to it all."
Ewan Robertson

From the very first lesson, a tutor will be assessing pupils' abilities and potential, getting to know each one as an individual, working out the best approach and the most rewarding avenues to follow. Not everyone knows exactly where they're heading when they arrive in Plockton, but they will get every chance to find out during their time at Sgoil Chiùil.

"Some kids are very mature and know where they want to go. Others don't know, they just want to play...You've got to take the balance. That doesn't happen overnight, it can take six months to fathom out. Then you've got to form a relationship with that individual for the student to get the most out of it."
Iain MacFarlane

Life in a residential music school is definitely a world apart, even with the broader spectrum of High School activities to balance it. The tutors' visits can be a welcome break in the weekly routine, a reminder of the outside world.

"It was tough going, you got cabin fever, and it felt "like a little bubble" after two or three years. It was very intense."
Suzanne Houston

"Sometimes...they're stuck in the Residence, stuck in school, then someone comes in and teaches a song or a tune, has a laugh...that's an important part of it."
Iain MacFarlane

Many tutors – through staying overnight, or getting involved in Centre activities – have become part of the extended Residence family. Some tutors have even stepped into regular roles, to help Dougie extend and develop the opportunities for students.

Karen Marshalsay and Jack Evans, both well-known performers, have cheerfully put in extra time to help with stage management at concerts. They involve the students as much as possible. The youngsters need to learn that life on the road is more than just turning up and playing. The stage crew are just as necessary as the musicians.

"Although we're well known as musicians and I'm quite well known as a producer, the kids get to see me moving microphones around, which is sometimes viewed as a fairly lowly operation."
Jack Evans

The Centre's library – one of the more elusive items on Dougie's wish list – has finally found a shape, thanks to Karen's attention. Jack spends many hours with Dougie in the studio, helping to produce the annual CD. In a vital contribution to the vexed issue of formal qualifications, Karen developed a joint assessment scheme for traditional music, in association with Trinity Guildhall (London). Almost every tutor has contributed to the immensely popular Music Weekends.

CHAPTER V

Music Weekends

Music Weekends are a chance to cover the many aspects of musicianship for which there is just not enough time in the weekly core curriculum. These include...music technology, stagecraft, theory, and contextual studies, all of which are essential parts of the skills set of any working musician.
Sgoil Chiùil Prospectus

Three weekends out of four are for going home, if students wish and if their journey is feasible – which it isn't for those from the Western Isles, Aberdeen, or Shetland, for example. Once a month everyone stays on for a Music Weekend, including the local day pupils. Staff and tutors get involved, and it's not unusual to find the Director joining in a joyful, noisy percussion session as the students explore the principles of rhythm.

"We do maintain that we're not a hot house for professional musicians, but we also want people to have the necessary

**skills should they require them. The Music Weekends focus
on the ancillary skills and experiences that any musician
needs in order to make their way."**
Dougie Pincock

Needless to say, one weekend in four isn't enough for everything
on the wish list, but it's amazing what can be packed into the time
available. At the start of the year there's often a weekend on basic
groupwork skills. The next could be about basic studio skills,
where students are introduced to the technical side of studio work.
There might be a weekend devoted to the hows and whys of solo
performance, or to stagecraft and live music – how best to use a
microphone, make introductions, present yourself, walk on and off
stage. Some themes come round every year, like the Burns weekend
in January.

**"It's always based around two things. One of them obviously
is Burns and his songs and work. The other is speed
groupwork, where students have between three and four
working hours to perfect an arrangement that has to be
performed at the Burns Supper that night. Then the Sunday is
a general Scots song event."**
Dougie Pincock

Specialised workshops and masterclasses from touring musicians
and music industry organisations are one of the highlights. They can
deliver a wealth of information – perhaps from the business world
of contracts, agents, managers, record companies, publishing deals,
copyright and intellectual property.

**"Another very successful one was a media weekend. Mary
Ann Kennedy and John Carmichael talking about radio and
TV respectively...That culminated in four groups making a
short radio programme and a short TV programme on the
Sunday...As well as being performers in a band, everybody
also took turns at being crew – cameramen, producers,
directors, runners, production assistants..."**
Dougie Pincock

There's also the chance of "a wee bit extra performance experience, because they get the opportunity to organise extra gigs". Particularly successful have been the song weekends, with the focus on Gaelic and Scots song. These mini festivals include concerts, workshops, visiting artistes, and are open to the general public.

> **"Obviously the young folk are involved in the performance side of that, but also in the production, front of house, CD merchandising...all the bits and pieces that go around a live performance...a couple of students have compèred those shows."**
> Dougie Pincock

The 2010 Singthing weekend brought together singer-folklorist Margaret Bennett, singer-storyteller Sheila Stewart, the Mick West Band, and the young musicians of Plockton. It surely doesn't come much more excellent than that.

CHAPTER VI

From Fireside to Classroom

Much of the teaching is carried out without the use of written music. There is a strong emphasis on oral tradition in Scottish music, and students are encouraged to develop ear and memory skills at every stage. Although written music is often used in learning, the material is invariably memorised whether it is learned orally or from the printed page. There is also a strong awareness of context and history in Scottish, as in most, traditional music, and tutors take care to make sure that students are made aware of the background, sources and history of the music they play. This extends also to contemporary compositions, and students are made to realise that they are part of a living and dynamic tradition which in addition to drawing from the past is constantly being refreshed.

Annual Report 2006/07

Fitting a hearthside tradition into an academic mould has been one of the most difficult challenges.

At four o'clock in the afternoon, the Residence springs into life as pupils stream "home" after the High School day. Suddenly the place is full of chatter, argument and laughter. Doors bang, Shona remonstrates, Dougie emerges from his office to shout reminders about things not done that should have been done. For the music students, the real work of the day is about to begin. They scatter to change out of uniform, drop off their school books and collect musical instruments. Then it's time for groupwork, followed by dinner, a brief interlude for TV or a game of pool, followed by music practice, homework, supper and bed. It's a long, full day.

But these are traditional musicians, whose music was always part of the fabric of life, woven into the rhythms and rituals of every day, month and season. Every task of the day had a song to accompany it – there were milking songs, rowing songs, lullabies, songs for spinning, weaving, reaping and sowing. Tunes passed naturally from father to son and mother to daughter. Young musicians knew the stories behind the tunes, and had a keen sense of carrying on the traditions of their parents and grandparents. Music was not a thing apart, rarefied or aloof. Excellence was nurtured right there at home.

"Earlier, especially in rural areas, everyone spent more time together, worked together and socialised together. The entertainment was shared with other people."
Iain MacFarlane

Sgoil Chiùil na Gàidhealtachd – where Dougie, his staff, the Residence team and the tutors encourage, cajole and nurture the wealth of talent in their care – has become a small community with music at its heart, a reflection of those earlier days when young people found their musical mentors among family and friends at home.

"Quite frankly, this music is no longer being taught in the community like that. People no longer sit round the fireside and pass on traditions. People sit round the playstation and the television. I'm not saying it's gone completely. I'm very glad to say there are still huge sections of this country where

**traditional music is taught in the old hand-me-on manner.
But there's less of it, and as it's dwindling you have to think
of something to replace it."**
Dougie Pincock

As the old way of life unravelled, its intimate traditions fell away
from a disintegrating framework. Fèisean nan Gàidheal threw the
first rope that helped rescue the music.

**"The way I see it, the Fèis movement, from a wee idea for
the kids to get the chance of having a go, has become the
foundation for kids not only getting the chance to see and
hear good players, spend time with them. They also meet
other kids from other areas, so it's like a big family....
Everyone's watching out for everyone else. I think it's
essentially how the tradition keeps going. Before the days of
Fèisean and Plockton and the RSAMD's traditional course,
there was nothing of that. So many people of my age group
that could have been players didn't have the opportunity.
There wasn't any kind of structure in place to make sure the
kids got a chance at it."**
Iain MacFarlane

What the Highland Council saw in the Scottish Executive's initiative
was an opportunity to build on what the Fèis movement had
achieved. Such a project, set in the secondary education system,
provided a stepping stone between the Fèisean and a number of
Higher Education courses that had arrived on the traditional music
scene. In 1993 the University of Strathclyde had started a BA course
in Applied Music, which included traditional music alongside
classical, pop and rock, and jazz. Across the city at the Royal Scottish
Academy of Music and Drama, a degree course in Scottish Traditional
Music was established in 1996. This was a big step. However, the rest
of academia was slow to acknowledge traditional music as anything
other than the domain of an eccentric minority.

**"The first time the traditional department was accepted
was at the Christmas carol concert in Glasgow cathedral.**

One of the clàrsach players did a traditional arrangement of Christmas carols for all the different instruments – clàrsach, accordion, pipes, fiddle, guitar, whistles – and it got a standing ovation! In the cathedral! After that we would get Visit Scotland phoning up wanting traditional music students to play at events for them. All of a sudden the classical students realised the traditional students were getting gigs and getting paid for them. That changed the attitude."
Ian Muir, Tutor, RSAMD

"The degree course at the RSAMD – I was one of the very first students to do it – was a statement for Scottish traditional music. It's given it status. I don't think we'll ever look back from that. The most important thing is that the community respect it, keep it true to the tradition."
Iain MacFarlane

The big challenge has been to stay true to the tradition while satisfying the demands of the education system.

"It's very hard to sit in a concrete room with the tutor and talk about Niel Gow – you should be in the living room beside the fire, peat burning away."
Iain MacFarlane

Having taken the step of bringing traditional music right into the classroom, the project team were determined to compromise as little as possible. They would stick to the time-honoured ways of teaching, though the hearthside lessons of old were long gone.

"We do try to adhere as closely as possible to the methodology that would be used if this were being taught in the community. If the place where youngsters are coming into contact with traditional music is school – as increasingly it is – then let's take advantage of that and do it in such a way as not to interfere with the crux of the tradition… You don't have to change your teaching methods to teach traditional music within the formal system."
Dougie Pincock

Dougie puts his finger on an important point, when he says that "oral/aural" doesn't mean "not taught". Excellence in traditional music (as in any other kind) has always been achieved through the highest standards of teaching, learning and practising.

> **"It is taught, but it's taught aurally and orally – and that's what we do. These guys teaching here, happen to be in a school. But if they were in a community, they would still teach the same way. The teaching methods are not changing – they use some printed music, aural instruction, a lot of singing, ear training. Quite often instead of giving the pupils printed music, we'll give them a recording and they'll go away, work with the recording and learn the tune by ear."**
> Dougie Pincock

The most difficult task for the tutors is to convey the spirit of the tradition so that the young players absorb it and bring it out in their own playing. They'll readily use modern technology to transform a weekly lesson into a constantly-available reference point. Voice recorders, CDs, computer memory sticks, MP3 players – all allow pupils to listen to their own playing or singing and compare it with original recordings that may not be technically perfect, but resound with the true meaning of the music.

> **"Luckily for me, I came from a family who were musical. Friends came to the house to play music. I was nurtured through the older generation like my father who have no technical training, but there's something in their music that you just cannot copy. You can't write it down on paper. That's the essence. I would like to say this is how you play it, then you put your heart and soul into it, and that's you playing the tune. That's the hardest thing to pass on."**
> Iain MacFarlane

Assessment and examination, those fundamental requirements of the formal education sector, have tested the ingenuity of the Sgoil Chiùil team from the start. Demonstrating the effective use of public money involves meeting requirements that can be an uncomfortable fit for traditional music.

> **"There is a problem with the presence of traditional music in the formal education sector...you have to tailor how traditional music fits and how it suits ways of examination for assessment and reporting...Formal assessment of traditional music is still hugely problematic in this country. There are major issues that have not been resolved and that have a long way to go before they will be resolved. It's been acknowledged at ministerial level for education. It's like turning an oil tanker – it's a long, hard job."**
> Dougie Pincock

A key figure in tackling this dilemma was Bert Richardson. Using his long experience as Advisor in Music to Highland Regional Council, and his involvement in developing the Standard Grade system, Bert suggested ways of integrating the needs of traditional music with those of the formal education system. The result was a bespoke system of assessment that met the criteria of the formal system without compromising the particular characteristics of traditional music. Once again, those involved were committed to excellence, whatever it cost them in time and effort.

The system is based – as might be expected – on oral rather than written assessment. Students record the same piece of music at different stages of the year – September, Christmas and Easter – which gives an overview of progress. They also record new, more demanding pieces, to make sure the task level is increasing at the same time. These recordings, along with students' project work and practice diaries, feed into the reporting process. Tutors write reports at Christmas and Easter, and the Director produces an annual report for each student at the end of the session in June. The system seems to work for all concerned, but assessment methods are being constantly refined, and the dialogue continues between NCETM, the Scottish Qualifications Authority (SQA) and Her Majesty's Inspectorate of Education (HMIe).

With regard to formal qualifications, there are more problems. Anyone wanting to take their music on to further study needs some kind of accredited qualification. Unfortunately, the requirements of the SQA are especially incompatible with traditional music. The major stumbling block is that the formal examining bodies insist on a written score that must be followed.

Pipers have always had their own specialist examiners. There is not a problem for them. Nor is there, most of the time, for a fiddle, whistle or accordion player who performs a tune. But anyone who plays an accompanying instrument faces a serious obstacle, as does a student who wants to present Gaelic or Scots songs for examination.

> **"In most, if not all, traditional music, accompaniment is improvised and there's no score – piano, guitar and clàrsach are very awkward. We can't let go of that without disadvantaging the players of those instruments. The other major problem is in song, where there are different views of grading a song. It is extremely difficult to get Gaelic or Scots songs approved for examination by the SQA. So Gaelic song is an acceptable topic, but trying to get material approved…I foresee this situation continuing for a while yet."**
> Dougie Pincock

Sgoil Chiùil's Director is determined that the core principles cannot be compromised, and that a mutually acceptable solution must be found. The situation took a big step forward in 2008, with the Trinity/Guildhall collaboration. Karen Marshalsay – harpist and clàrsach tutor with a wealth of educational experience – was impressed by this organisation's attitude towards traditional music.

> **"The main thing is they accept that traditional music is a performance of the moment – about composition during performance, about small subtleties…They would still like to see a notated version to give the examiner an idea of the starting point, but the actual performance is marked as just that, not a performance of what's on a piece of paper."**
> Karen Marshalsay, Tutor

The First Class – the nine intrepid pioneers. From left: Ruairaidh Campbell, Ishbel Strachan, Jane Slater, Zoë Renouf, Gillian Fleetwood, Katherine Kemp, Gillian Chalmers, Calum Beaton, Ewan Robertson.

"Good enough to attract the seals!" An early session on Calum MacKenzie's boat.

Yes, they do smile on stage sometimes.

A rhythm workshop using human crochets and quavers!

"If you can't play it in the practice room you can't play it on the stage."

"And what a beautiful place to study!" S6 students at work in the library.

A big adventure – Celtic Colours, Cape Breton 2003.

The end of an era – Bert Richardson retires.

"A singing teacher will drop in on a groupwork session…"
A Gaelic song arrangement comes together.

"The other side of the teaching fence." A primary school workshop on the big tour.

"And just one more, please." Another album in the making.

In the big boys' playground – on tour with the Sorley MacLean project.

"Where does this bit go?" The pre-gig setting up ritual in action.

The Gentlemen's Tea Party; tea just out of shot.

Marianne comes home – workshop at Spean Bridge Primary School, June 2009.

"The emotional pinnacle."
Celtic Connections Festival, Glasgow Royal Concert Hall January 2010.

The great benefit was that these examinations – which for most instruments take the form of performance certificates – were already validated. At last, traditional musicians, including accompanying instrumentalists and singers, could take grade examinations while remaining true to their own tradition. This was an enormous improvement, achieved only after a huge amount of work on Karen's part. Perhaps even more demanding – and more rewarding from Karen's point of view – was her creation of a full set of Joint Assessment Grade Examinations for clàrsach. These carry the same weight as the full classical grade examinations, and required the invention of a whole suite of supporting tests and technical work.

Such is the dynamism within Sgoil Chiùil that Karen's success led swiftly to another exciting development. The driving force this time was the school's Acting Course Leader, Becky Milne, herself an accomplished musician.

Becky arrived at Sgoil Chiùil in 2007 as Evening Supervisor, a position that combined two of the Centre's three core strands: music and welfare. With the development of a new sixth year course in General Musicianship, she wove the third strand – education – into her contribution.

It had always been felt by some people that graduates of the National Centre of Excellence in Traditional Music should leave with some kind of recognised qualification. At the same time, there was a growing desire to broaden and deepen the students' learning experience. With the best will in the world, talks and workshops at monthly Music Weekends were never going to provide more than a frustrating glimpse of the possibilities – and the gaps were being noted.

"Feedback from the tertiary establishments when we were sending people out…great players, good work, good in the studio…not too bad at the context and history side of things, but poor on the actual music theory and musicianship, harmony, transcription and analysis."
Dougie Pincock

"One of my main concerns – I don't mean Plockton particularly – is some of the students don't have much general theory knowledge. RSAMD have introduced a basic theory test once the students have been accepted. If they don't pass, they'll get a short sharp course to get them up to speed."
Ian Muir

A new module in Harmony and Accompaniment was somehow squeezed into the Sgoil Chiùil curriculum, and Theory joined the list of second study options – attracting a surprisingly large number of students. Then came the opportunity to build these and other elements, such as sixth year projects, into a properly-designed course with staff to run it.

"The S6 course has drawn together a number of already existing but quite disparate strands of what we were doing. The biggest achievement was to make things happen in a formal, structured way, which had previously been happening in a haphazard fashion."
Dougie Pincock

Becky devised a course in two parts for the sixth year (S6) students. For the first half of the academic session, up to Christmas, they follow a teaching programme that covers music literacy, harmony, the background to traditional music, and specialist talks by tutors. From January the focus is on individual projects, undertaken with support from the staff and tutors. Through a remarkable piece of collaboration with Plockton High School, an extra six hours of music teaching has been incorporated into normal school hours as a timetabled choice. All High School students choose their sixth year studies from five columns divided into a number of subject options. The High School have "donated" to the Music School one option from one column, which gives Sgoil Chiùil's S6 pupils exclusive access to General Musicianship as part of their general programme. This effectively increases their basic ten hours' music study by over 50% – a massive leap.

The first students enrolled on the new course in August 2008. It was pronounced a definite success. However, laurels aren't for resting on at Sgoil Chiùil, and the start of the 2009/10 session witnessed a further level of excellence, thanks to a fortuitous and productive meeting with Mary MacDonald and Jane Rimmer of the SQA. Mary and Jane spotted the potential for a link with the SQA's newly revised National Certificate system. Normally delivered through colleges and further education establishments, this course meets SCQF Level 6 (equivalent to Higher Grade). It is a full-time syllabus of 12 free-standing units – equating to approximately 12 hours of teaching per week.

With just half that time available, was it possible to match six units from the National Certificate in Music with those already included in the Plockton course as developed to date? It was. Careful selection resulted in the adoption of *Appreciation of Music; Music: Live Performance (ensemble); Performing Music on One Instrument or Voice (solo); Music: Listening Skills; Music: Literacy*; and the *Creative Project*. They were an almost perfect fit. The revised course began in the 2009/10.

Supervision and support are provided on a day-to-day basis by the Course Leader, with specialist input from visiting tutors. The six units are internally assessed within the Centre, with external moderation from the SQA.

Once again, the tutors are fundamental to the teaching programme. The tutor talks enable greater in-depth study of specialist subjects with all those taking the S6 course. Pupils gain an insight into the different traditional instruments and the various types of music and song. Every talk is followed up with set tasks that help fix the new knowledge.

The creative project is an exciting venture for the students. They work individually, devising their own project on a topic that reflects their personal connection with the traditional music of Scotland – they could research the music and song of a particular area, turn a collection of tunes into a book and CD, produce a written piece about a musical subject of personal interest, gather tunes and songs from a family background, make a demo album of their own performance, or a printed collection of their own compositions. Such a variety of topics hones an enormous number of skills, from studio recording, to research methods, to fieldwork. It takes the students (often literally) beyond Plockton, and brings them into contact with other people and places, giving them a taste of the different roads they might travel in future.

As the course develops, students will receive an official qualification, equivalent to half the National Certificate in Music, as well as their completed project. The award is an impressive component of any CV and comes from a unique course within a unique institution.

> **"Although the National Certificate in Music is available in a range of institutions, this is the only General Music course taught within the language and environment of traditional music."**
> Becky Milne, Acting Course Leader

Needless to say, Sgoil Chiùil have their eye on the full National Certificate for their students. That would mean 12 hours' teaching per week, which would require a slot in two S6 subject columns, or delivery over S5 and S6.

The current six units are particularly relevant to students already committed to becoming musicians. With a broader choice of units, the course could appeal to a wider range of students, whose further and higher education might include music but not necessarily centre on it. The benefits extend well beyond paper qualifications.

> **"The contribution of the course to the students as musicians and people is huge."**
> Becky Milne

Six extra hours spent in the Music School allow time for more thought about what they are doing there. Many students already have a strong sense of themselves as "tradition bearers". Extra time in the company of the tutors allows them to understand and talk about where their music came from and how it fits in with other traditions. They can strengthen and validate their own sense of identity within the tradition. They can also reinforce earlier learning, explore beyond familiar boundaries and establish strong musical literacy. Feedback suggests the course is certainly a hit with the students.

Listening skills –

"…it's never been a strong point with me…I could practice a lot more at it…especially identifying intervals by ear…I didn't know quite enough…I found it difficult…I just need some more practice…"
S6 Course Feedback, Dec 2009

The tutor talks –

"…they really know what they are talking about…so much information and history passed on…learning more about other genres……more tutor talks and for longer… learning a lot more history and information…I want to know everything…"
S6 Course Feedback, Dec 2009

If pupil enthusiasm is any measure of success, this initiative takes Sgoil Chiùil into the next decade with a good chance of meeting the fireside-to-classroom challenge.

CHAPTER VII

Give Me Band Names!

Groupwork is a core part of the Centre's work. Although there is a high level of individual instruction, the nature of traditional music is such that most performance is done in ensemble, and this is true of the performances of the Centre's students.

Annual Report 2006/07

At the beginning of each year students are grouped into "official bands", the primary aim being a good musical balance of instruments, as well as a harmonious combination of experience, age and personalities. The groups meet between four and five o'clock every afternoon, Monday to Thursday. It's important that any non-resident pupils don't miss out, so they stay on after the High School day and the Centre makes sure they get home safely afterwards.

Dougie takes a particularly active interest in groupwork, seeing it as one of Sgoil Chiùil's special strengths. His students would seem to agree. For most it's a new adventure. One young piper, whose previous experience was solo competitions, pibroch and pipe bands, declared that playing along with different instruments was much more fun.

> **"You have to play differently...the chance to have a tune... just make music."**
> Chris Waite, former student

Sgoil Chiùil's groupwork in a residential setting lays the foundations for making music with other people. A fiddle player can pick up a whistle and try it, an accordionist can find out about a clàrsach. What's more, coming as they do from all over Scotland, the Plockton students have plenty opportunity to learn different tunes and styles from each other as well as from their teachers. Understanding what other people are trying to do is a vital aspect of playing in a group.

> **"That's one of the real positives...other students have to get into that way of thinking – how to play with a fiddle player, or a piper."**
> Ian Muir

The groupwork experience certainly stands them in good stead when they have the chance of music-making elsewhere, and Sgoil Chiùil's graduates are quick to find such opportunities.

> **"On average they're much more successful at doing that immediately they get here. Our other musicians maybe take a year and half, two years to have the confidence to do things on their own."**
> Gerri Rossi, University of Strathclyde

Neil Ewart enrolled on the Strathclyde Applied Music course and got involved in Glasgow's music through listening and playing in weekly bar sessions. He happened to meet up with another former Plockton student, Suzanne Houston, they entered the Danny Kyle Award competition in 2008 and much to Neil's astonishment, were one of the six winners.

"Groupwork made a massive difference to me. By fifth year I'd got involved in group organisation as well, which was good experience."
Neil Ewart, former student

Back in Plockton, the official bands are expected to select a repertoire, arrange music to suit the instruments in the group, and to perform their work in public. They have a great deal of autonomy, though Dougie, his Groupwork Supervisor and the nominated lead tutors oversee the evening sessions and are always on hand to help resolve problems. If there's a disagreement or two, it's treated as a taste of life as a real musician, something to be sorted out for the sake of the music and the band as a whole. This is one of the advantages of living together in the Residence. Students quickly learn that though it's not possible to get on with everyone, you learn to live alongside them – an experience that not every young musician will have when they step out into the wider world.

Groupwork isn't always about making music. Sometimes there's a chance to listen, widen the horizons a bit, maybe take on board some new ideas and try them out.

"Plockton broadened my musical perspective...Instead of just Martyn Bennett, Shooglenifty...Dougie said listen to some of this older stuff, and it just blew my mind, some of the stuff that had been done 20-30 years ago."
Ewan Robertson

If band members want to try something new, they'll get full support, on the understanding that only the best possible result will do.

"...the whacky ideas that youth would come up with. We never got a 'no'."
Neil Ewart

"Time and again, our students alternately amaze me and drive me to despair with their incessant creativity and invention. As the ideas get more outlandish, I'm torn between whether to stamp them out or throw more coal on

the fire. Usually at that point, Jack reminds me that we're here to make the students' ideas reality, so the coal goes on and you get to hear the results."
Dougie Pincock

Discussion, suggestion and constructive criticism are all part of the process. And if at the end it simply doesn't work, Dougie won't hesitate to let them know. If he says "the guitar's not working, get rid of it," he's commenting on the arrangement, not the guitarist. The process of giving and receiving advice is not personal. It's all about learning to be excellent.

"Dougie...would tell it the way it was, he wouldn't beat about the bush...There was no mollycoddling at all. If you were playing badly he'd let you know, but positively, show you how to put it right. That was a huge thing for me, just trying to get better, to mature in my music."
Ewan Robertson

Each band has to come up with its own name. Strangely, this seems to cause more difficulty than any other part of the work. It's not unusual, amid the scramble to get ready for the first gig of the year, to hear a roar from the office: "I still need band names!" On occasion, the Director has been seen marching up and down the aisle of an imminently-departing bus, muttering. "Band names, give me band names."

And so they have materialised over the years:

Aspograss • Secret Circus • Ma tha mo Thogair • Spunkie Clooties
Untouchables • Heeliegoleeries • 4 O'Clockitis • 'S Math Sinn
Dolly Mixtures • Procrastinators • Faulty Dynamite
Gentlemen's Tea Party • Na Dudaichean • Dead Stop

CHAPTER VIII

Practice Makes Excellent

Evening practice is monitored, and usually a tutor is present to assist as appropriate. Students are encouraged to practise both individually and together, and are very supportive towards each other in the learning process. The use of practice diaries enables the supervisor, the tutors, the Director and the students themselves to monitor progress continuously.
Annual Report 2006/07

> **"If you can't play it properly in the practice room, you can't play it properly on stage."**
> NCETM Student Handbook

The authors of the Student Handbook know what they're talking about – they've put in the hours of going over and over a piece of music, a phrase, a tricky run of notes, up and down the scales. They know what it takes to practise not only until you can get it right, but until you simply can't get it wrong. "Do a warm up," they say. "Start with the bits you find hardest; start slow; set goals; be organised…"

It's six o'clock in the evening. For music students, the brief after-dinner interlude is over and it's time to get back to work. One of the most important alterations to the original asbestos-ridden building was the creation of nine custom-made practice spaces. Most years there are more music students than spaces, so the hours between six and seven o'clock and eight and nine o'clock are allocated for music practice, with everyone having one timetabled hour for each. From seven to eight o'clock is time for High School homework.

Such complex dovetailing helps integrate the two residential populations of Music School and High School students. It looks rigid on paper, but the evening staff on duty in the Residence will go out of their way to accommodate a change or two if, for example, students want to join in sporting activities. But the practice hour will be there, somewhere, at some point in the evening.

"Practising is more than just playing through a few tunes"
NCETM Student Handbook

Without practice nothing works – the groupwork, the recording sessions, the performances. Very often much of the toil seems to have little to do with actually playing a tune, but it leads eventually to the joy of fluency and the fun of making good music with other like-minded people.

"When you sit and watch a band playing…you can watch really accomplished musicians having fun and you think it's all fun. I think a lot of the younger ones don't realise that a lot of hard work goes into getting to a level where you can just enjoy it."
Iain MacFarlane

For each of their two studies, students will have work set by their tutors. Sometimes lessons are recorded, and the student will work from the recording, perhaps trying out the tutor's suggestions for improvement. Maybe there's a new technique to learn, or a tune to work on for a future performance. Scales, exercises, chords, fingering, bowing – an hour can pass quickly...or slowly, if things are not going well.

With excellence as ever the goal, such demanding practice sessions can be a challenge for young players, but help is never far away. Evening practice is supervised, supported as much as possible by tutors and Dougie. And of course there's always next week's lesson, where a troubled student can find reassurance that it's all worth the effort.

> **"Music adds to your character...a great therapy altogether. I wouldn't survive without it!"**
> Iain MacFarlane

Then there's the Practice Diary. Every student has one. Over ten years, the concept has evolved into a personal record of musical progress and self-appraisal. It has become part of the official assessment process, helping the tutors and Dougie to compile their student reports. Just as important is the Diary's role in forming good practice habits.

It's a faithful, if nagging, companion. Which instrument did you practise this evening? What did you do? How did it go? Is it getting better or are there difficulties? How can you improve? Be specific!

> **"The more specific you are in your entries, the better you will understand how you best learn, find out what ways of solving problems have worked, and see your progress"**
> Practice Diary instructions

Self evaluation isn't easy at any age, but Sgoil Chiùil's young musicians quickly learn to lend a critical ear to their own playing.

> **"Practised chords in F... Triplets on guitar... Fiddle, vibrato, all three fingers... Must get good at triplets... Crunluaths, five in a row without mistakes... Didn't get good at triplets... Listened to recording of song from lesson... Triplets – aaah... Fiddle practice went well"**
> Practice Diary entries

Practice hour over, the Diary written up, it's time to find a supervisor to sign it. Administrative overkill? No, this is a fundamental part of the assessment and support system. Without the Practice Diary, a huge part of the student's musical progress would be missed. The practice supervisor's signature comes with a chat about the day's entry, suggestions for how to get over obstacles, perhaps an additional note that Dougie or a tutor could offer advice. At the end of the week, all Practice Diaries are handed in for the Groupwork Supervisor to read. Any significant problems noticed will be passed on to Dougie, who will work with the supervisors, the student, the tutor – whatever it takes to help get past the stumbling block and smooth the way forward.

"It'll take you more than a night to get good at triplets – keep going!"
Director's comment in Practice Diary

Even the tone of a Diary entry can point to something not quite right. Does someone sound down in the dumps? Perhaps the Residence staff can shed some light, or maybe there's a bit of stress on the academic side. Everyone is constantly aware of the pressure, and whatever the trouble, no pupil need struggle alone.

For most students, the formal practice sessions will be just a tiny part of the work. At weekends and in spare moments, enthusiastic pupils may experiment with new tunes, learn a new song, perhaps compose something of their own, exploring musical ideas and discussing repertoire with their groupwork band. Sometimes they will simply be exhausted and want to sleep or catch up on television programmes – and that too is alright. It's all part of the journey towards sharing excellent music.

CHAPTER IX

Music is for Sharing

In the traditional music school, the pupils benefited from a very focused development of their performing skills... pupils were highly motivated and committed to pursuing an interest in Scottish traditional music. They worked effectively together in groups to prepare arrangements for public performance.

HM Inspectorate of Education report 2004

While not every Sgoil Chiùil pupil is aiming for a career as a professional musician, the essence of traditional music is in sharing it with others, whether informally with friends or on a floodlit stage with hundreds of people.

"Usually about three times a year there'll be some kind of performance element to the Music Weekends. The Christmas concert, the end of term concert, the S6 tour in March, and the tour in June – all are additional to the Music Weekends

and are specifically performance based. Over the course of the year the Centre undertakes around 35 to 40 performances. So, especially the senior pupils, they do get a tremendous range of performance experience before they leave here."
Dougie Pincock

Plockton's young musicians grow into confident performers. They've been meticulously trained by people with extensive experience of performing. They know that it involves much more than standing on a stage, playing a tune. It includes introducing what you're going to play, connecting with the audience, setting them at ease. Nervous performers make an audience apprehensive. People want to sit back, relax and simply enjoy the music. They need to feel the performers can handle the occasion.

"Dougie knows what it is to sit in a teaching room and teach, and he knows what it's like to be in front of 1,000 people, performing. That's the difference, being able to do both."
Ian Muir

The tutors too are seasoned entertainers, guiding pupils steadily towards their public appearance. From lesson to practice room to groupwork session, every step leads to the performance, any performance – the more frequent and varied, the better.

"We've had people at Celtic Colours in Cape Breton, the ladies' lunch club in Portree, the Traditional Music Awards, Tartan Day in New York, Glenelg senior citizens' Christmas lunch..."
Dougie Pincock

No matter who, or what, or where, the young musicians learn to treat every audience, every programme, and every venue with the same respect.

"Each one has to be treated professionally, handled differently – some have big sound systems, big stage crews.

**At others it'll be down to the students to do everything
– they decide how long to play for, assess the audience,
balance the material. It's a huge part of their professional
development – people skills as well as musical ones."**
Dougie Pincock

It's quite a test for the carefully-developed bond between the
musicians themselves. This is the point at which the group must
hold together. Any cracks, any hesitation, and the audience will lose
confidence and not enjoy the concert. Then – the tutors and Dougie
might say – you won't be asked back, and out in the big, bad world
where good traditional musicians are ten a penny, you need to be
asked back. You want to be the band that's remembered – and for
the right reasons – the performer everyone wants on their stage. You
have one chance to make your mark. If you have 40 minutes on stage,
you have to make every one of those minutes count. The shorter the
time, the more vital each minute. If you go to Celtic Connections, or
Tartan Week, you're going to be playing alongside some very big
names and you want people sit up and take notice. If you're doing a
gig in aid of the local hospital, you need folk to open their purses and
give generously. That means coming up with the goods, and nobody
else can do that for you. What you have to do is get up there, engage
your audience and play better than you've ever played before. Every
single time.

**"The best integrating experiences are the performances,
the gigs. That's what bonds the team very quickly. They get
thrown in, they have to survive, they've got to do it."**
Dougie Pincock

And they do survive. And they get asked back. And their path is
strewn with accolades, friendship, laughter – and occasional banana
skins.

September – minutes before the start of a concert, one of the
students discovers he's left behind a vital part of his pipes. They are
unplayable. Everyone else is ready and getting increasingly anxious.

Will they have to re-arrange the whole programme? The desperate piper waves his fellow musicians on to the stage, and several tense minutes later he joins them – having somehow cobbled his pipes together. Piper and pipes survive to the end of the concert, which is a resounding success. The audience was blissfully unaware of the piper's self-inflicted difficulties.

December – it's chilly in Kintail village hall. The young musicians of Sgoil Chiùil have just arrived to prepare for a concert to raise funds for the local children's Christmas party. The hall keeper turns on the heaters and lines up chairs for the audience. The stage crew of tutor Karen, supervisor Becky and some of the students are busy setting up the stage. Traditional music has entered the electronic age with its microphones, speakers, tangles of cables and ear-splitting howls as the sound system is tweaked into place.

Dougie has positioned his mixing desk near the door, ready to deal with the howls and balance the sound. He calls for a sound check, and a small group – fiddles, a guitar, a clàrsach, whistles – comes on to the stage. They tune up, then gradually move into a set of reels until they are in full flow. Suddenly one of the fiddlers wavers, loses confidence, and the tune dwindles to a halt. Dougie calls a suggestion from the back of the hall, encourages another try. No good. Self-doubt has taken over. "I can't do it." Without hesitation, a fellow fiddle player steps in. "Watch me. We'll play it slowly, like this…and again…again, a bit faster." The faltering one tries, succeeds, relaxes. "We're ready, Mr P." The sound check continues. During the concert in the evening, the stumbling block passes without a hitch and everyone grins, including Mr P in his dark corner. Excellent.

May – the village of Dornie basks in evening sunshine. The audience is gathering for a concert that includes Skye and Lochalsh Junior Pipe Band, the Strath Gaelic Choir and students from the National Centre of Excellence in Traditional Music, as part of Scotland's Year of the Homecoming. Special guest performers will include former Sgoil Chiùil pupils, Ewan Robertson and Gillian

Fleetwood, two veterans of the Centre's very first year in 2000. Ewan was voted BBC Radio Scotland's Young Traditional Musician of the Year in 2008. Gillian – a Danny Kyle Award winner – is here with Fraya Thomsen as The Duplets, their successful clàrsach and song duo.

The tiny backstage space is crammed with musicians tuning up. Gillian Fleetwood is paddling happily in Loch Long. "You're on in five minutes," shouts Dougie Pincock from the door of the community hall. A faint "it'll be fine", drifts up from the edge of the water. Dougie sighs. Ten years ago, Gillian's catch phrase was a saving grace during those first difficult months of commuting between Plockton and Skye. Right now, her former Director is thinking that "jump-to-it" would be more appropriate. But she's a first-class musician, a delightful person, and will put on a great performance with Fraya – if he can get her to the stage on time.

He does, and it's fine.

Either way, Dougie knows "the audience doesnae care" about his troubles. It's a lesson he drums relentlessly into his students. A professional musician cannot survive without an audience. People pay to be entertained, it's the musician's job to entertain them, and the audience simply doesn't care if the bus was late or a fiddle string has snapped or the piper forgot a bit of his pipes – or one of the guest performers has gone paddling...

> **"The gigs and the stage work made a big impact. Dougie helped prepare us for the real world with the hands-on approach while we were young. It was scary at first, though!"**
> Neil Ewart

> **"Having to get involved in setting up the rig is good experience. Now I can hire a rig and set it up myself for a gig. It saves money."**
> Chris Waite

One by one, glamorous illusions are dispelled. What could be more exciting for a musician than taking to the road in a big van and touring the country, making music, visiting exotic places, meeting interesting people? Twice a year a group from Sgoil Chiùil leaves Plockton in a big bus, for the students to experience the full repertoire of touring: the anticipation, the boredom, exultation, exhaustion, food good and bad, the waiting around – for traffic to clear, hall keys to materialise, sound equipment to co-operate, instruments to go missing and be found. Of course, there's also the camaraderie, the great music, the satisfaction of meeting the challenges. The main tour takes place in June, preceded by the S6 tour in March, each lasting a week.

> **"As an education project, we always like to have some kind of educational aspect to these tours as well. In most cases that takes the form of visiting a school, which is near where we're playing, or it might even be where we're playing. We visit the school during the day and we do some kind of workshop or performance based thing depending on what they think would be the most beneficial thing."**
> Dougie Pincock

For a short time, the Plockton students learn how it feels to be on the other side of the teaching fence. Everyone agrees that it's an intense, challenging, and immensely rewarding experience.

> **"It puts our students on the spot. Sometimes we have to react quite spontaneously. We don't know what the standard of the players in the school's going to be like. If it's a good standard, then we quite often have to think on our feet and have rather more of a session than a workshop."**
> Dougie Pincock

Sometimes there have been forays abroad, to Cape Breton or Brussels, for example. In 2006 one of Sgoil Chiùil's official bands crossed the Atlantic for Tartan Week, an initiative by the Scottish Government to highlight the Scottish presence in New York. Neil Ewart, Seàn Gray, Colin Masterton and Chris Waite – The Gentlemen's Tea Party – found themselves playing in the concourse of Grand Central

Station with two of the biggest names in Scottish traditional music: the Peat Bog Faeries and the Finlay MacDonald Band. With typical generosity, these seasoned performers encouraged and supported the young musicians. Finlay MacDonald even gave them a slot during his band's evening gig. It was a brilliant, never-to-be-forgotten professional experience for those involved.

> **"Going to New York for Tartan Week was the single best motivation I gained from Plockton…I felt like a real musician, flying over, staying in a swanky hotel…going to gigs and jazz clubs…"**
> Neil Ewart

> **"Tartan Week was an amazing experience…playing among such big names as Peat Bog Faeries."**
> Chris Waite

At home in Plockton, Sgoil Chiùil has become a local "big name", thanks to Dougie's policy of bringing the students out into the local community.

> **"Probably in the first two years, no-one knew it was there because it was so new. Everyone wondered, what's that attached to the school? Gradually the students came out to play at various functions. Everybody was amazed. Very soon they got to know there were top musicians coming to Plockton."**
> Charlie MacRae, Chairman, Plockton Community Council

And so the music flows, from the village hall –

> **"If you want some music, phone up Dougie and if they've got a free date they'll come and play…For them playing in the village hall offers them experience, being away from the school."**
> Charlie MacRae

…to the Plockton Inn, where live traditional music is always on the menu, and after the Christmas and June concerts, students and their parents congregate. Of course their music comes too.

> **"They will play and people are stunned. The students with their instruments – pipes and whistles and fiddles – they're all multi-talented."**
> Kenny Gollan, Plockton Inn

...to boat tours in Plockton Bay –

> **"A few came down on a Sunday when they were at a loose end and played on the boat. The passengers were gobsmacked at the standard of playing and the enthusiasm... The seals particularly enjoyed it, some came very close to the boat. They were good enough to attract the seals!"**
> Calum MacKenzie, Seal Boat Trips.

The young music makers have gathered fans on the doorstep –

> **"I think it's the best thing that's happened in Plockton for years...They don't only play in the school, they play charity concerts, the old folks home...I don't think there's anyone who doesn't know the school's there, because of Dougie's enthusiasm as much as anything."**
> Dick MacRae, weaver, who lives at the end of the school drive

...and from farther afield –

> **"People know of the music school abroad...it brings people from all over the world to Plockton. The music school has put Plockton on the map."**
> Kenny Gollan

For the students, it's simply about playing and sharing the music they love.

> **"Performing is natural for them, that's what we do for them."**
> Dougie Pincock

Ten Years, Ten Albums

The students of Sgoil Chiùil na Gàidhealtachd make an album every year…The process provides the students with a professional quality experience of the recording studio, and prepares them for what can often be a daunting part of a musician's life.

NCETM Prospectus

A proper recording studio was high on Dougie's list of priorities right from the start. He knew how important such a facility would be – things had changed since his first endeavours as a musician.

> **"You used to get your wee band together, and make up your music and play it a wee bit in your bedroom, then you took it out and played a wee gig here and there, then maybe a couple of festivals and a wee tour. You worked your way up with the live playing, until you had a sufficient repertoire of sufficient quality to perhaps aspire, one day,**

to step into a recording studio. That was the top of the
mountain. Nowadays, the recording studio is base camp.
Instead of using the gigs to get the recording, you now use
the recording to get the gig. That's alright if you make a good
recording, but if you make a bad recording then people are
not going to be very interested in booking your band."
Dougie Pincock

Before they leave Sgoil Chiùil, every student is able to handle studio
equipment, with its buttons, sliders and microphones. That opens
doors on future career choices. It also makes the musicians aware of
the difference between a live performance and playing in a recording
studio. First and foremost, they learn how to make a good recording.

"Today it's absolutely essential and fundamental for students
to have knowledge of the technical side of music."
Gerry Rossi

Dougie wants good studio musicians as well as good live performers.

"The focus is on learning how to play the music in a studio
situation. Because the wall doesn't clap or cheer, you have
to learn to play in a sterile environment, to play so that it
sounds good on repeated playings because usually you have
to make several takes, and it still has to sound reasonably
fresh. There's a compromise between what sounds exciting
and full of mistakes and what is very correct but not very
exciting. There's also knowing your part so well that you can
overdub as an individual, without the rest of the band. Being
able to play in time and in tune – both have to be better in
the studio environment."
Dougie Pincock

Most of the recording takes place during study leave in May and
June each year, with recording days arranged round students'
examination commitments. Everyone has vivid memories of making
the CD, and all judge it to be one of the most valuable experiences of
their time at Sgoil Chiùil.

"A great idea. We learned how to play for recording, which is completely different. It was strange at first but a big help. It also gave us a taste of handling equipment in a studio."
Fiona MacAskill, former student

"The album is one of the best things. You're very exposed, you can't hide behind the rest of the band as you can when performing. The experience of a real-life situation prepares you for the future. You get blunt feedback during these recording sessions if it's necessary. You learn not to take it personally...it's for the music."
Suzanne Houston

Dougie doesn't disguise the gruelling nature of recording a CD. Reality is hammered home by devoting long, intensive, exhausting days to the process. Yet laughter is never far away. One of the most essential pieces of equipment turns out to be a specially-prepared "survival box", whose contents include high-energy food and drink, spare strings, and "the worst smelling deodorant in the world"!

Given the restrictions of CD space and recording time, priority is given to the official bands, with solo/duet performers and informal bands getting the chance if possible. Inevitably there's far more material than can be used, and Dougie has to make difficult choices.

"I'd love to put everything in but it's just not possible. We've had to leave out some really good stuff because there simply isn't enough room on the CD."
Dougie Pincock

In recent years, there has been a double album – and still there's not enough room! Mixing the CD during September and October absorbs a huge amount of time and concentration on the part of Dougie and Jack Evans, without whose invaluable assistance the task would be impossible. The sleeve and label are designed by a local graphic designer, and students get involved in selecting photographs, writing sleeve notes, and choosing the title – a task almost as agonising as the quest for band names.

First Class · Duck! · We're a Case, the Bunch of us
The Biggest Folk Band in the World...Ever!!!
Three Cheese and a Teaburger · Now That's What I Ceòl Music!
May the 4th be With You · Enjoy the Ride · The Rugby Goalie

The tenth album – yet to be named – will be launched in the usual tradition, at the Christmas concert in mid-December. It's always a proud moment for the young musicians when they see – and hear – the results of their efforts. The CD acts as a publicity tool for both the students and the Centre. Complimentary copies are sent to a wide range of media contacts and people associated with the Music School. As a commercial venture, it generates a small trickle income, which goes towards such things as instrument strings, reeds, meals on trips...and good coffee for the Director and his staff. This last is much appreciated by the pupils, who quickly learn the benefits of caffeine for their elders.

> **"Dougie put in a huge amount of work on making the CD, but it was best to avoid him BC (before coffee)!"**
> Chris Waite

Recording isn't restricted to the main CD. Some S6 students also choose to make an album as part of their personal project, getting a second bite of the CD-production cake. And the studio comes into its own at several points throughout the year, as an aid to monitoring students' progress as performers. The individual September, Christmas and Easter recordings make important contributions to the annual reporting process by tutors and Director.

> **"The quality of the annual CDs, and the production – having the studio here – is very high. That's a great resource, a real contribution to the cairn of Scottish culture."**
> Duncan Ferguson

CHAPTER XI

Show Time!

The Plockton Centre already undertakes an extensive programme of performances, and all of the four Music Centres which come under this funding are in regular contact with each other...The National Showcase of Excellence...is now established as an annual feature of the Centres' work.
Annual Report 2006/07

Since 2005, November has been National Showcase time, a major highlight of the calendar for Scotland's Centres of Excellence in music. This is a unique experience for the young musicians of Sgoil Chiùil na Gàidhealtachd, the City of Edinburgh Music School, the Music School of Douglas Academy, and Aberdeen City Music School. For one intensive weekend, the traditional musicians of Plockton join their mainly classical counterparts in a public celebration of all that is best about the whole Centres of Excellence project. It's a perfect opportunity for the youngsters to learn about each other's music. It also poses significant challenges for those who devise the programme.

"The four Directors of the Centres all have some knowledge of each other's music but not in depth. Putting programmes together has been a very interesting experience. It's been interesting to see how other people do things, other methods of putting on a gig. It's been a very good learning experience for all of us. Certainly for the kids, it has been a real eye opener from both aspects, classical and traditional. We at Plockton have done some things to tailor for these showcases that are not necessarily what we would put on in a gig – clàrsach trio, accordion trio, piping trio, trying to make it palatable for a mainly classical audience."
Dougie Pincock

One inspired innovation was a competition for Scottish composers. The two winning commissions, scored for both classical and traditional instruments, were performed as the finales of two consecutive Showcases. The challenge gave the young musicians much to learn in a short space of time. Not only did accordionists and clarinettists, pipers and trombone players find themselves playing side by side, but they also had to work with the composer and a specially-selected professional guest conductor, to prepare the new work for its world première. Their excellence was well and truly tested, and they emerged with flying colours, year after year.

In each Centre, the weeks leading up to the event are frantic, with planning, preparation and rehearsals squeezed into whatever gaps can be found in the packed weekly schedule. At last there's just time for one final run-through before the musicians take to the road. At Sgoil Chiùil, anyone who happens to be in the residence is rounded up and ushered into the music room. There's hardly room to play a fiddle, let alone a set of highland bagpipes at full volume. Dougie acknowledges the less-than-perfect circumstances, but he expects a professional performance all the same. Within the limits of the cramped surroundings he gets one, though the audience consists of a handful of tutors, supervisors, Residence staff, and passing writers. The Director has generous praise, thanks and encouragement for the students, who have given so much already and now have a big occasion ahead of them.

"You've put in the work. Just keep the heid and you'll be fine. Enjoy it."
Dougie Pincock

Then he slips into parental role, running through a checklist of music, reeds, fiddle bows, vital pieces of bagpipe, spare strings, the right stage clothes, not forgetting the black socks, black shoes, black trousers (no jeans, not even black ones) – and Sgoil Chiùil shirts. Cathy Taylor remembers the hated task of ironing those shirts.

"If they were going away, it would be 'oh please miss could you iron this shirt?' And I said have you not done it yourself yet, come with me and I'll show you. 'Oh no miss, you're much quicker.' I'd have a queue at the door once I got the iron going. I didn't mind because I'd rather see them smart going out and I felt kind of responsible."
Cathy Taylor

The four Centres take it in turn to organise the National Showcase of Excellence. In 2007 it was Sgoil Chiùil's turn. They chose the Spa Pavilion in Strathpeffer as a venue – big enough for a good-sized audience and a large group of performers, with good backstage facilities, plenty of parking, easy access, and in a town with ample overnight accommodation for all those musicians and attendants, parents, guests, bus drivers... Of course, the place was 60 miles away from Plockton and on the other side of the country – just one more administrative challenge!

The commission competition had been won by freelance composer, Lila Senior, an accomplished violinist and pianist. Her orchestral piece, The Boat of Mannanan, was inspired by a Celtic legend. It was a big, dramatic work that placed considerable demands on the young orchestra, but they had an impeccable guide in Garry Walker, taking time out from his commitments as Principal Guest Conductor of the Royal Scottish National Orchestra and the Royal Philharmonic Orchestra.

> **"Garry was an absolute star. The kids loved him. He seemed to have a way of relating to them, of bringing stuff out of them that they didn't really know was there...He was incredibly demanding but backed it up with praise. When they were doing it right he let them know they were doing it right, and when they were doing it wrong he let them know that as well. But he also let them know how to fix it."**
> Dougie Pincock

Throughout the rehearsals, Garry was clearly confident that he would get the result he wanted. He did, and it was superb.

> **"I had the pleasure of doing a showcase concert with the students from the four Centres of Excellence. We had great fun, and they were super to work with. The standard of the playing was really high, but what particularly impressed me was their level of commitment. We did a piece commissioned especially for the occasion which was far from easy, and involved clàrsach, pipes, accordions and orchestra; ergo, not easy to put together, as all these instruments respond in different ways. The performance was a real success, and the Plockton contribution was a tribute to the good teaching of their staff, the excellence of the students and the spirit of the school. May the next ten years be as profitable. And what a beautiful place to study!"**
> Garry Walker, Guest Conductor

As one Showcase follows another, standards creep ever upward, communication grows between the four Centres of Excellence, and musical boundaries tumble.

> **"The first Showcase had an atmosphere of the unknown. The second one was better, people were able to integrate and talk to each other more. At the third one in Strathpeffer, everyone stayed under the one roof for the first time. After**

the concert we had a bit of a ceilidh. As you'd imagine, our guys took the lead because it's what they know, and the others really threw themselves into it. They danced, played, sang songs. It was fantastic. That has now broken down the barriers...the Showcase has been one of the best things that's happened from the Centres of Excellence project. It's got these young folk together realising the value of what each other's doing and what they're doing themselves. It's given everyone a sense of their own relative worth."
Dougie Pincock

By bringing together the four Centres in one very public event, the Showcase goes beyond the personal benefits to those involved. It is also a tangible, exhilarating, and inspiring demonstration of what the Centres of Excellence project has achieved on a national level. No written report could match it. The "national" aspect is important, for these publicly-funded institutions have a double-barrelled remit. They are not just centres of musical excellence – they are National Centres of Excellence in Music, and they need to operate in the national arena.

It would be easy for Dougie and his colleagues to lose sight of the wider world as they focus on nurturing their talented pupils. In turn, the world outside could readily overlook a small, specialist school tucked away in a remote corner of the north-west Highlands. Dougie works hard at the two-way process of remaining alert to what's happening in the real world of traditional music, while fostering a high profile for Sgoil Chiùil across the length and breadth of Scotland and beyond. Rarely a day goes by without telephone or email communication with several people on his extensive and growing list of contacts. Hardly a week passes without tutors bringing news fresh from the live music scene beyond Plockton.

Geographical remoteness is not allowed to be a barrier. From their secluded niche, Plockton's young musicians travel throughout the country and wherever they go, they have a three-pronged ambassadorial role – for Plockton High School, for Sgoil Chiùil na Gàidhealtachd and for the Centres of Excellence project itself.

"It is important for you to remember that everywhere you play now you are associated with and effectively represent the National Centre of Excellence in Traditional Music."
Student Handbook

The association continues beyond their time in Plockton. For ten years, graduates of Sgoil Chiùil, like generations of Highlanders before them, have been making their way south to the opportunities offered by city life. Two destinations in particular draw the young musicians to Glasgow – the Royal Scottish Academy of Music and Drama (RSAMD), and the University of Strathclyde. The RSAMD runs the only course in the world that leads to an honours degree in Scottish traditional music, offering "a unique training for individuals wanting to make a career in traditional music". The University of Strathclyde's degree course in Applied Music covers "all styles and genres of music – jazz, traditional/folk, rock, pop and classical", aiming to equip its graduates with "an in-depth understanding of all aspects of the modern music industry."

In a remarkable tribute to the work of Sgoil Chiùil, the people running these two very different courses are in complete agreement about the quality of students who come to them from the National Centre of Excellence in Traditional Music.

"I have to say I don't know where the traditional music course here would be, without Plockton. They are the main feeder for the Academy course...it's been an absolute joy having people from Plockton. They can play, and they're nice kids as well."
Ian Muir

"Plockton is very firmly established in the area of traditional music...it's like a jewel to have a school like Plockton...Our relationship with Dougie and the team is really important, because they will give us recommendation and advice... When I ask students to send in a recording, we always include a reference form for the teachers. We're looking for performance, academic potential, technology awareness.

When we see an application coming from Plockton with Dougie's report, we have an understanding of that student... It makes our job easier."
Gerry Rossi

Closer to home, Sabhal Mòr Ostaig is an internationally recognised centre for Gaelic language and culture, where all teaching and administration is conducted in Scottish Gaelic. Founded in 1973, the College is an academic partner of the University of the Highlands and Islands Millennium Institute. Their programme includes a degree course in Gaelic and Traditional Music (BA Gàidhlig agus Ceòl Traidiseanta), which has attracted several students from Plockton.

All these educational opportunities, and others further afield, require academic credentials as well as proven musical ability. Thanks to Sgoil Chiùil's work with London-based Trinity Guildhall, and the Scottish Qualifications Authority, students will soon be able to set out on the next stage of their career with a recognised qualification from their time in Plockton.

There's no doubt that the Centre is now a full-time player on the national stage, where traditional music is concerned.

"Sgoil Chiùil na Gàidhealtachd comes from Scottish Government through Highland Council, which has Culloden as part of its patch and also the Music School at Plockton as one of its cultural treasures. It's part of the Scottish cultural landscape now."
Duncan Ferguson

AFTERWORD

Dougie Pincock

The Celtic Connections concert was without doubt the emotional pinnacle of my time at Plockton. It really did feel during those 50 minutes that all the tribulations of the last ten years had been worthwhile. The ten students on stage delivered the performance of their lives, and the atmosphere in the room could have powered the National Grid.

But as Sir Isaac Newton and Oasis have somewhat differently observed, we stand on the shoulders of giants, and those ten youngsters couldn't just have been parachuted in there at any point in history and done the same thing. Lists of thanks are notoriously dry reading and usually read only by those who know they're going to be thanked, but that doesn't make them any less valuable, and in this case, the old saw of "we couldn't have done it without you" is actually true.

There are lists of tutors and people who have given workshops as appendices to this book. They read like a Who's Who of Scottish traditional music. We have been so fortunate that these people – busy professionals themselves – have bought into the idea of Sgoil Chiùil and given so much of their time, energy, and priceless knowledge to our students (and, I may say, each other).

A residential project needs a residence. Right from the word go, Cathy Taylor, Shona McGuinness, and all the staff who have come, gone, and stayed, have risen to the challenge of the extra demands that our students bring with them. The greatest tribute to them is the number of students who come back and say they didn't realise how good they had it until they left!

Our students have to go to school. Anybody who's ever changed school will know what a traumatic experience it can be, for parents and pupils, and Plockton High School has coped incredibly well with the challenges we have thrown at them.

As you'll know if you've read the whole book this far, Sgoil Chiùil na Gàidhealtachd had a difficult birth. They might not appreciate the analogy, but without the midwifery skills of Bert Richardson, Laurence Young and Duncan Ferguson, there wouldn't be a book to read or ten years of a music school to celebrate.

There are many others to thank – parents and families, politicians, councillors, council officials and staff, the other three Music Schools, schools we've visited, gigs we've done, audiences we've played to, people who've bought CDs, journalists, photographers, artists we've supported, the local community. The sheer number of people we've somehow managed to come into contact with never ceases to amaze me, and they've all made their contribution.

It's often invidious to start naming individuals, but some people make such big contributions that they must, in fairness, be acknowledged.

I couldn't have done what I have, for good or ill, without the support and patience of my own family. Gillian, Eve and Duncan have all spent a lot of time waiting for me over the past ten years, and I can't begin to say how much that has meant to me.

This book owes its existence to the tolerance, patience, persistence, enthusiasm and skill of Terry Williams. She hasn't just written it – she's lived it.

Ronan Martin has been involved from the very start, and pretty much any visual image you see which concerns Sgoil Chiùil has had his hand and eye upon it.

The photographs in this book were taken by Nigel Butterworth, Anita Hurding, Iain Johnston, Cailean Maclean, Alastair Scott, John Sikorski, John Slavin, Terry Williams, and possibly some other people to whom I apologise!

Amid the chaos that tends to ensue when I get an idea, somebody has to keep an eye on the mundanities of making sure the place continues to exist. Sarah Houston started that ball rolling, and more recently Becky Milne has been a one-woman oasis of reason and calm. But no-one has done more in practical terms to keep the whole edifice propped up than Anita Hurding, and whether they know it or not, everyone who's dealt with us over the past seven years owes her a debt of gratitude to some degree – but no-one more than me.

And finally – they exasperate me, they take up loads of everyone's time, they forget stuff, they disappear at inopportune moments. But they also impress me. They work hard, they're talented, they're keen, they're (usually!) pleasant, and even while I'm upbraiding them, I'm always admiring them. Because if they didn't buy into it and they didn't come, none of us would be able to enjoy the fruits of their labours. And the future of Scotland's music would be a little less bright.

I would like to thank, and dedicate this book to, the students, past, present and future, of Sgoil Chiùil na Gàidhealtachd, the National Centre of Excellence in Traditional Music.

Dougie Pincock
Director, NCETM
March 2010

Applying for a Place at Sgoil Chiùil na Gàidhealtachd

Admission to the Centre is by audition, and successful candidates are expected to show a high standard of performing ability as well as evidence of genuine potential to develop as traditional musicians. The application and audition process is very straightforward. Applications close at the end of February or in early March each year, and auditions are held in late March. Applicants are notified before Easter whether or not they have been successful.

There is no fee to attend Sgoil Chiùil na Gàidhealtachd. There are no academic standards to be met. But the challenge of winning a place is formidable. The first step is to visit the Centre. An Open Weekend is held annually in February, offering the chance to meet staff and students, ask questions about the Centre, and to have an advisory audition with the Director. Individual visits and auditions can also be arranged throughout the year, as mutually convenient.

At an advisory audition, the Director listens to a prospective applicant playing and advises on the likelihood of their being accepted. You have to be pretty good in the first place, and then you have to have the potential to become pretty excellent too. It doesn't mean you have to have lots of certificates and prizes or high grade examination results. It does mean you need to show conviction and commitment through your playing and through talking to the panel at your interview.

With vacancies at a premium, places at Sgoil Chiùil are not offered lightly. Open days, and especially advisory auditions, act as a relatively painless filter. Then, in order to be considered for a full audition, candidates must make a formal application.

At the full audition, the applicant is asked to perform 15 minutes of music of their own choice. A short interview follows, after which the applicant's parents or guardians are invited to meet the panel and ask any questions they may have. The auditioning panel consists of the Director, a senior management representative from Plockton High

School, a specialist in the applicant's first study discipline (usually the relevant NCETM lead tutor), and the Highland Council's Music Development Officer.

Applicants who pass the final audition are invited for an induction week in June. This gives a brief experience of life as a student at the Centre. At the end of the week each student has a short interview with the Director, at which it is mutually agreed whether or not the student will take up their place. Successful applicants then commence their studies at the Centre the following August.

If you do come to Sgoil Chiùil na Gaidhealtachd, it's very likely that you'll have a wonderful experience, make incredible progress, and remember your time in Plockton for the rest of your life.

For full details of how to apply for a place at the National Centre of Excellence for Traditional Music / Sgoil Chiùil na Gàidhealtachd, contact:

The Director, NCETM
The Residence
Plockton High School
Plockton
Wester Ross,
IV52 8TU

01599 544706
dougie.pincock@highland.gov.uk
www.musicplockton.org

Ten Years of Tutors

This list includes all the people who have provided one-to-one tuition at the Centre, at some point over the last ten years, either as regular lead tutors or occasional deputies. Tutors are listed under their main instrument, but they may have taught other instruments as well.

Accordion: Blair Douglas, Sandy Brechin, Gary Innes, Kathleen Boyle, Ross MacPherson, Alasdair MacCuish, John Carmichael

Cello: Wendy Weatherby

Clàrsach: Ingrid Henderson, Karen Marshalsay, Bill Taylor, Marie-Louise Napier, Eilidh MacLeod, Corrina Hewat, Deirdre Graham

Fiddle: Iain MacFarlane, Gordon Gunn, Duncan Chisholm, Charlie McKerron, Lori Watson, Jenna Reid, Pete Clark, Bruce MacGregor, Louise MacKenzie, Aonghas Grant

Flute: Hamish Napier, Iain MacDonald, Rebecca Knorr, Nuala Kennedy, Kevin O'Neill, Niall Keegan

Gaelic Song: Mary Ann Kennedy, Wilma Kennedy, Rachel Walker, Julie Fowlis, James Graham, Arthur Cormack, Margaret Stewart.

Guitar: Jack Evans, Jim Hunter, John Saich

Piano: Andy Thorburn, James Ross, Mhairi Hall

Pipes: Iain MacFadyen

Scots Song: Christine Kydd, Mick West, Maureen Jelks, Alison McMorland, Sara Grey, Emily Smith

Whistle: Dougie Pincock, Marc Duff

APPENDIX III

Ten Years of Workshops

These people have done Music Weekends or workshops – some have been more than once. They are listed in chronological order of their first visit. Tutors listed in Appendix II may also have provided workshops, though not mentioned here. The Director apologies for any omissions – they are purely his responsibility.

Corrina Hewat
David Milligan
Michael Marra
Kathleen Graham
Tony McManus
Alyth McCormack
Mary McMaster
Alasdair Fraser
Paul Machlis
Cliar
Back of the Moon
Dannsa
Fred Morrison
Ross Martin
Ann and Charlie Heymann
Susie Petrov
Hollis Easter
Nancy Groce
Beolach
Clan Terra
Eira Lynn Jones
David Sumblow
Kieron Means
Jimmy MacBeath
Geordie MacIntyre
Colcannon
Donald Black
Malcolm Jones
Andrea Larsson Attanasio
John Goldie

Iain Fraser
Iain Lowthian
Christine Hanson
Marc Clement
Anne Martin
The Chris Norman Ensemble
Rod Cameron
Simon Bradley
Luke Plumb
Steve Kaufman
Sandy Stanage
Savourna Stevenson
Chris Stout
Fraser Fifield
Catriona MacKay
Malcolm Stitt
Dochas
Anna Massie
Jenn Butterworth
Mairearaid Green
Sandra Joyce
Kath Campbell
Fraser Stone
Angus Grant
Peter Daffy
Tony Ellis
Doris Rougvie
Terry Day
Sylvia Barnes

Margaret Bennett
Aaron Jones
Claire Mann
Billy Jones
Barbara Dymmock
Scot Gardiner
Geordie Murison
Joe Aitken
Donna MacRae
Martin Hadden
Matt Seattle
Christine Primrose
John Carmichael
Val Bryan
Paul Anderson
Shona Donaldson
Maeve MacKinnon
Frank McLaughlin
Ali Hutton
Willie Beaton
Mairi Sine Chaimbeul
Wilfar Mathieson
Neil MacRae
Duncan MacInnes
Tim Kliphuis and Swing
Karen McAulay
Tom Spiers
Jamie Laval
Michael Bryan
Andy Irvine